More Praise for *Ingenuity*

"What an insightful, provocative, and practically helpful book this is! Lisa Thompson not only illustrates how and why Black women struggle to find acceptance and recognition as preachers; she also posits multiple ways in which these women preach with risk, imagination and ingenuity, offering specific examples from their sermons. In addition she identifies strategies whereby any preacher who has been labeled as "other" can craft sermons that defy the norms of conventionality, while also honoring the best of their traditions. A great book for both personal and classroom use."

—**Leonora Tubbs Tisdale**, Clement Muehl Professor Emerita of Homiletics, Yale Divinity School, New Haven, CT

"Writing from the deep well of the spirituality of black women, Thompson has given us a remarkable guide for what preaching should be and must be for the times we are in. Accessible, thoughtful, probing, pastoral, prophetic—all come together in this text. A must read for anyone committed to faithful excellence in proclaiming the word."

—**Emilie M. Townes**, Dean and E. Rhodes and Leona B. Carpenter Professor of Womanist Ethics and Society, Vanderbilt University Divinity School, Nashville, TN

"Lisa Thompson has written an absolutely essential book for every preacher and student of preaching. With power and precision, with brilliance and grace, she mines the creative genius of black women's preaching for homiletical wisdom widely missed and long overdue. Accept her invitation to take a seat at this table and listen. Attend carefully to the intonations of the outsider. It will open up worlds for all of us."

—**Anna Carter Florence,** Peter Marshall Professor of Preaching, Columbia Theological Seminary, Decatur, GA

"In this ground-breaking book, Lisa Thompson attends carefully to the actual sermons of black women who preach in order to distill principles and best practices for *all* preaching. The book is scholarly, energetic, clear, and practical, providing many new insights for preaching in every context. Highly recommended."

—**John S. McClure**, Charles G. Finney Professor of Preaching and Worship, Vanderbilt Divinity School, Nashville, TN

Lisa L. Thompson

ingenuity

Preaching as an Outsider

Nashville

Ingenuity:
Preaching as an Outsider

Copyright © 2018 by Lisa L. Thompson

All rights reserved.

No part of this work may be reproduced or transmitted in any form or by any means, electronic or mechanical, including photocopying and recording, or by any information storage or retrieval system, except as may be expressly permitted by the 1976 Copyright Act or in writing from the publisher. Requests for permission should be addressed to Permissions, Abingdon Press, 2222 Rosa L. Parks Boulevard, Nashville, TN 37228-1306, or permissions@abingdonpress.com.

Library of Congress Cataloging-in-Publication Data has been requested.

ISBN 978-1-5018-3259-8

Unless noted otherwise, scripture quotations are from the Common English Bible. Copyright © 2011 by the Common English Bible. All rights reserved. Used by permission. www.CommonEnglishBible.com.

Scripture noted as NRSV are from the New Revised Standard Version Bible, copyright © 1989 National Council of the Churches of Christ in the United States of America. Used by permission. All rights reserved worldwide. http://nrsvbibles.org/

for those who dare to move in foolish courage . . .

contents

ix   Acknowledgments

xi   Preface: The Question(s) in the Room

1   Introduction: #PerceivedOutsider

     2   Personhood and Pulpit Personas
     5   Faux Pioneering in the Ministries of Black Women
     6   Resetting the Rules of Engagement

11   Chapter 1: When Bodies and Unimaginative Practice Collide

     12   Black. Woman. Preacher.
     15   The Limits and Dangers of Unimaginative Practice
     16   The Collision of Unimaginative Practice with Real Bodies
     19   An Act of Constrained Invention

23   Chapter 2: Ingenuity for the Sake of Proclamation

     24   Preaching as a Communally Defined Practice
     26   Proclamation as a Marking Experience
     28   The Black Preacher as a Ghostly Image
     32   A Practice That Opens and Generatively Disrupts
     34   Imitating, Mimicking, and Preaching
     35   Communal Choreography and Sacred Vibrations

contents

37 Chapter 3: Mining Life for Preaching

- 39 Connections and Bridges to Life
- 40 (Re)Imaginings of the Familiar
- 52 Ingenuity and Everyday Life
- 53 (Re)Imagining Sermon Development
- 61 Using the Familiar as a Resource

63 Chapter 4: Recovering Sacred Texts for Preaching

- 65 Interplay and Play
- 66 (Re)Imaginings of Texts
- 84 Ingenuity and Interpreting Scripture
- 86 (Re)Imagining Sermon Development
- 104 Creative Intelligence and Interpretation

107 Chapter 5: Finding "A Word from the Lord" for Today

- 110 Very Present Truth
- 112 (Re)Imaginings for Here and Now
- 122 Ingenuity and Truth Telling
- 124 (Re)Imagining Sermon Development
- 136 Immediacy Textured

139 Chapter 6: Locating God and Faith on the Ground

- 141 A Very Present Help
- 142 (Re)Imaginings of the Ordinarily Sacred
- 156 Ingenuity and the Story of Faith
- 160 (Re)Imagining Sermon Development
- 172 Sacred Storytelling

173 Conclusion: Risk-Taking for the Sake of Life

- 174 Leaving Space for Possibilities
- 175 Cultivating Risk-Taking for Ingenuity
- 176 Preach, *Regardless.*

- 177 Notes

acknowledgments

This book would not be possible without the women whose sermons are major thinking partners for this text. Your ministries and voices are powerful. I cannot name the value of what you've entrusted to me through the vulnerability of your gifts and calling. Continued blessings to you and your God-given voices. And this immediately tangible work is a result of the labor and patience of my editor Constance E. Stella, and the Abingdon team, including Peggy Shearon, Laurie Vaughen, and Jeffrey Moore. Your willingness to wrestle with my ideas for the sake of imagery, religious practice, and scholarship has made this a better book.

There are ebbs and flows in the life of writing and teaching, and I've had a wise group of people who could see down the road ahead of me. Serene Jones, president, and Mary C. Boys, dean, at Union Theological Seminary in the City of New York afforded me the space and support required to bring this project to fruition in its final and most critical phases. Evelyn Parker, N. Lynne Westfield, Debra Mumford, Andrea C. White, William H. Myers, and David Esterline knew when to push me and when to tell me to rest.

This book had its early germination during my graduate studies. John S. McClure was adept at reading and honestly commenting on my fledgling thoughts with record speed, helping me better shape and crystalize them; thank you for being a continued trusted advisor and supporter. Dale P. Andrews, left us too soon, but his memory leaves a lifetime of imprints; thank you for showing me glimpses into the life of a scholar by way of being an accessible mentor and friend.

acknowledgments

My colleagues have been graciously supportive and encouraging along the journey. I am forever indebted to my lifelong Vanderbilt connections (including Black-Vandy, H&L, and T&P friends), members of the Academy of Homiletics and its Black Caucus, the Association of Practical Theology, the Society for the Study of Black Religion, and the Wabash Center for Teaching and Learning in Theology and Religion. Many others have created space for me to lecture, teach, and preach over the years. I do not take these opportunities for granted—as they are often the place where I've publicly worked through the ideas on these pages. Thank you to those who call me their teacher. You afford me the honor of being a lifelong pupil.

My family by kin and friend has sustained me on this road. Kim, Carmen, Ariel, Heather, and Candis, thank you for doing the work only the women can do. My siblings are the consummate shoulders on which I lean: Erika, as an exceptionally biased cheerleader, you keep me believing. Eric, you keep me pragmatically dreaming. Necole, you keep our hearts open. None of this would be possible without the sacrifices of my parents. Jettelean Geraldine Womack Thompson and Joseph A. Thompson, your vision was often ahead of your era, but you showed me how to take risks, *regardless*. Thank you for entrusting the dreams and drive of the ancestors to your children.

I give my deepest thanks to all of you, named and unnamed.

preface
The Question(s) in the Room

Let me begin by addressing the questions head on. From the inception of the work that led to this book, I've been asked one question over and over, "Why will people who aren't black women care about this?" And admittedly I became more perturbed every time I was confronted with the question. The answer I wanted to give went something like, "I can't believe you're asking me this question in 20XX! Is there nothing others can learn from black women? For eons and often without question, people have made generalizations about all sorts of things from the thoughts and ideas that presume the presence of white men." But alas, here, at the preface and end of this work, the gist will be the same but less curt, and intentionally so. I will *partially* relieve you of the burden of trying to determine if this book is for you.

"Why black women?" The easy response is, "Why not?" When black women surface as the subject of conversation and when the subsequent questioning follows this very push-pull underscores the attention that the conversation demands from everyone. Because some *bodies* have long been credited conversation worthy without warranting the question, "Why?" There remain factors in the context of our world, and particularly in the US, that connect the stories and experiences of black women even as those experiences differ from one another. The joys, burdens, and complications placed upon black women's personhood remain both vaguely and strongly tethered to an economic building of our country based on the free and forced labor of black people. This history of captured and forced labor, while not the beginning of black womanhood, shaped and continues to shape the lived realities of black women's economic, physical, mental, and relational well-being. Black women still make up the majority of black Christian worshipping communities, and theses contexts of faith remain significant for those women. We only need to take a look through the windows of rural, storefront, mega-, and televised church services to witness this reality. There remain significant connections between the contemporary world and the ongoing lives of black women, religiosity, and faith.

"Why preaching?" The pulpit literally and symbolically wields a great deal of power in communities of faith. The pulpit is sometimes the space of preaching, and the ability to occupy it signals the authority granted a person to shape belief within a community. As it shapes belief through preaching, the pulpit is often the space that recirculates the air of beliefs and ideologies back into a community. In the best of circumstances, preaching brings fresh air and contributes to the ongoing living and thriving of individuals in ways that are healthy and work together for our human flourishing. In the worst of circumstances, preaching recirculates polluted air that is connected to troublesome social histories and relationships that eventually lead to the demise and erasure of some persons and ultimately communities. Therefore, part of the work in preaching is determining how to filter out the polluted air, even when we exist in communities and in a world that often do not recognize that the air is tainted.

"Why black women and preaching?" Black women remain some of the least regarded individuals in our world and still struggle for inclusion in both our social and religious conversations. Some religious spaces still block women's access to preaching and the pulpit by outright denial or denying ordination. Ordination and preaching are not necessarily the same, yet neither are they mutually exclusive. Even spaces that do not block the official preaching of women often function in ways that give preference to the lenses of men and whiteness. Some black religious and preaching traditions have relied on prefacing a people's survival and well-being through creative engagement with a faith and world that is shaped as anti-black.

preface

Yet, while there are avenues afforded for imagination and creativity for the sake of life, creativity and imagination have not always been afforded for the lives of black women. Attending to the lives of black women calls us to reshape both our view and practices of preaching. When we consider the thriving and well-being of black women as primary, it affords an opportunity to consider how a distinct group of people often denied full personhood helps us rethink our approach to biblical interpretation and the process of proclamation. For we do not truly gain fresh air in our communities until we attend to the most vulnerable and they, too, can breathe untainted air, courtesy of speech that shapes our behavior and beliefs for the wellbeing of our body politic.

"Why now?" The process of cleaning up the air in communities of faith often requires creative resources and wisdom about how to navigate the technology of those communities (sacred texts, faith claims, meaning making, and worship practices). Once individuals gain exposure to less contaminated air and experience breathing anew, they are more adept at noticing tainted air when they move about in other spaces. Preaching as it is still valued within communities of faith is one means by which we potentially change the way in which we live together within these communities and in the world. Even in a world that screams post-religious and post-Christian, our current state of affairs proves the loose yet powerful influence of religious rhetoric that is named Christian and its ability to shape our public lives. The only way to explore the possibilities for the way in which Christian rhetoric, theologies, and beliefs have the ability to shape our lives together for the better is through the concrete exploration of how our beliefs land upon concrete bodies and their lived realities. So here we are with the opportunity to rethink preaching through the lens of black women, for their making creative use of the technologies available to them through Christian preaching practices; this is for the sake of their overall well-being and thriving in a world not built for their thriving. In this present moment, we may gain a glimpse into ways of moving forward that contribute to social change for the sake of our lives together, right here and right now.

preface

"For whom is this book?" This book unapologetically supports the work, ministry, and thriving of black women. We have long neglected black women in texts about preaching that focus on best practices, assumptions, and methods. To deny the distinctiveness of black women's social location as it relates to religious practice is to carry forward irresponsible exercises in the production of knowledge. This book gives primacy to the preaching of black women within spaces that expect preaching to take a form continuous with some sense of its historical scaffolding in black Christian histories. This is a book for black women. Yet, as this book is unapologetically about the ministries of black women, it also without question assumes that others have a great deal to glean in conversation with black women. However, such a back-and-forth exchange requires our willingness to come to the table in an attempt to understand a conversation that does not first center our concerns. The opportunity to apprehend and understand that which is other than we are is a privilege; it guarantees to reshape our own thinking and practices in ways we do not know until we take a seat at the table.

"How should I sit?" Some of you have been sitting at this table for a long time; I invite you to listen for a different pitch and bring the vibrations of your experience to these pages, allowing them to intersect and comingle with the ideas from the outset. Others of you will be arriving at the table for the first time; I invite you to a posture of listening in momentary silence. If you are struggling to find yourself on the page or locate your story, refrain from the urge to insert yourself and your primary needs upfront. Chime in, interrogate, and probe for relevance only after you can articulate an understanding of what has been stated. If you attempt to insert your needs too quickly you may miss the opportunity present or the real texture of the conversation taking place.

"Who am I?" All of our work is autobiographical in one form or another, whether we overtly acknowledge it or not. I acknowledge how I enter this work. I am a black woman. I am a preacher. I traveled the sometimes bumpy path to preaching and ordination in communities connected to black protestant Christian traditions that did not always fully affirm the presence of women. I preach and minister across various

preface

communities of faith, including those closest to the ones that most shaped my early belief and those farthest from those communities in both hue and tradition. I am a professor. I had the privilege of access to higher education. People allow me into their most intimate moments of struggle to find meaning and name it. I am trained in critical thinking for the purposes of shaping arguments and teaching; and I believe that these processes have merit for our life together. I am a daughter, a sister, a niece, a sister-cousin, and a granddaughter connected to enslaved, sharecropper, and free traditions of the North Carolina South. I am shaped by the deep wisdom, knowledge, and lives of women and men to whom I am indebted forever. While this book is absolutely not my autobiography or simple reflection, this book is strangely about me as much as I resist it. I try to lift up the voices of different preaching women, honor their preaching ministries, and construct an understanding of preaching in conversation with their work; and still, my personal interests and hope of holding together collective wisdom for the sake of the lives of black women direct the thoughts and ideas on the page. You will feel the tussle for this multivalent conversation through tonal shifts along the way. My voice pushes forward in places where the preachers themselves might not have gone. I cannot deny this reality. Pushing and constructing is my work and the work of this book. Whatever epiphanies and stumbles present in this text, I know to whom I am accountable and invite you to hold me accountable to our collective wisdom. Let us begin.

introduction
#PerceivedOutsider

In 2013, we saw the rise of the hashtag #BlackLivesMatter (BLM). And by the fall of 2017, we saw the rise of the hashtag #MeToo, although its inception came in 2006, long before its climb to the forefront in the media. In between both of these hashtags were the cries of #SayHerName, which is a part of the campaign of the African American Policy Forum.[1] The monikers were not just pithy sayings, social media capital, or signifiers of "woke" status. To the contrary, the hashtags claimed a particular type of shorthand for the violence and invisibility rendered to black bodies, not exclusive of black women, as these violent acts intersect with the historical social, economic, racial, and gendered location of women of the black labyrinth[2] in North America and beyond. In short, the undervaluing and disregard for black life and black women's lives in particular lead to the grotesque treatment or ignoring of black women's lives. Our ignoring such atrocities is being called to task.

The aforementioned hashtags represent movements created and led by black women. Two of the movements were quickly co-opted and credited to people who were not black women. #BlackLivesMatter was started by Patrisse Khan-Cullors, Alicia Garza, and Opal Tometi. The very compilation of their trifecta exemplifies the labyrinth of black identity in the US. Two of the women self-describe as queer-identifying, and one of the women comes from a Nigerian-immigrant family. Despite the founder's identities, BLM was quickly mis-accredited to men of the movement. Likewise, #MeToo was dubbed by Tarana Burke in 2006, intending to draw attention to survivors of sexual violence experienced by women of color and those belonging to lower socio-economic classes. The movement was quickly credited to white wealthy women of Hollywood, to the extent that the creator herself was not included in the cover photo for *Time* magazine 2017 Person of the Year campaign entitled "The Silence Breakers," which paid homage to #MeToo. Black women being cut out of their own *herstory* and the rewriting of history are not new practices.

Each hashtag, even their attempted co-optation, underscores both the fragility of black women's lives and the sin of systems that afford black life to constantly hang in the balance at the discretion of others. What is most intriguing is the fact that faith communities were not at the forefront of these social movements, or their actions were often met with suspicion. The fault is none but our own, as faith communities are often culpable of rendering the same crimes in our houses of worship. We've committed these sins in ways that are impossible to tell if we have let the crimes of the world seep under our door or if our crimes have seeped out into the world.

The question that begs to be answered is, how does our religious discourse reinforce or disrupt such ideas around black personhood and black womanhood in particular? A more important questions is, how do we lean into listening to those closest to the forced positions of marginality proclaim and declare faith in ways that disrupt such death-dealing assumptions? #MeToo, #SayHerName, and #BlackLivesMatter call the pulpit back to a faith-filled responsibility that attends to the deepest ills of society, and in their best practices, faith communities call the world to task about its crimes against the creation of God. However, before faith communities can move outward, we must first look inward to the places where we ourselves have stumbled on the gospel. We must look inward to the places where we discredit the belonging, credibility, and personhood of black women on a regular basis.

Personhood and Pulpit Personas

I am reminded of our crimes from the words of colleagues, students, encounters with random strangers, and those I know well. Doing or not

introduction

doing whatever some think they mean by *black preaching* or even *women's preaching* is risky business. Black women are always subject to the assumption made by other people that they have the power to accept or reject black women's ways of moving about in the world. White students have walked up to me to report what my white colleagues have told them, such as, "Professor XYZ said the sermon you preached in chapel was good, but it wasn't like your last sermon; and in the last one you did *black preaching*." The perceptions of listeners are often warped by gendered and racist stereotypes of both performance and one's personhood or lack thereof. These biases are not limited to white spaces and white bodies, neither are they limited to good or ill intention.

"I don't like women preachers." A senior and well-respected woman in the community spoke these words directly to me as I exited the pulpit. She was one of several people who enveloped me in curiosity, encouragement, and prayer during that time of ministry in Los Angeles. The congregation was historically traditional and African American. The community had never ordained a woman and did not afford women the opportunity to preach proper, although women did plenty of preaching via testimony and speaking. Therefore, "women preachers" did not exist much around those parts. This well-intentioned church-mother followed her short and sharp statement with a slight grin of approval, saying, "But I like you. You don't sound like a man, but you don't sound like a woman either." Somehow I had managed to accommodate her subconscious and yet-to-be-named assessment of an appropriate balance between femininity and masculinity, for bodies that looked like mine and offered their voices from pulpit spaces.

I have yet to decide if I feel more offended, flattered, or indifferent about her complexly androgynous description of my pulpit persona. Regardless of my personal feelings, the words were a genuine account of her experience. Her words also illustrate the connectedness between marvel and offense when we attempt to account for the presence of black women in relation to preaching. Questions of the ability, place, and authority of a black woman to name something significant on behalf of a community are often the backdrop for the delight taken in the word experienced and proclaimed. Internal discord surfaces within us when an unexpected something happens: "I don't like women preachers. But I like you." In these instances, as listeners, we now have to reconcile our experience with our latent assumptions. And as those who proclaim, we have to sit with the reminder that people do not readily believe our voices belong at the table; our status is often that of forced outsider.

I wish random encounters in congregations and academic hallways were where the echoes of our crimes stopped; but alas, they follow us all the way into the classrooms of our seminaries and divinity schools. In 2014, I posed a question to a group of students in a course on African American preaching traditions. As part of the course requirements, students brought sermon clips to class every week, yet none provided sermons by black women. At the end of the term, my question to the group was, "Why not?" The answers included: "They act and sound like men," and "I don't like them (their preaching)." But the most troubling and honest confession was, "They don't have anything substantive to say." Full stop. Once again black women were the "they" and "them" treated as peculiar objects and pushed to the periphery of the preaching conversation and our very classroom.

The responses were like a bad song on repeat. I was not surprised by the responses. I was surprised people were willing to be honest about their deepest beliefs, as they had sat eagerly with this black woman as their professor an entire term. The disheartening reality was that the responses came from women. These same women had just finished preaching, while fighting to find their voices and wrestling for words that mattered. The men remained complicit in silence except for one hesitant soul who said, "I've heard men preach bad sermons too."

In a graduate-level classroom ancient assumptions about women, black women's personhood and femininity, and black women's ability to speak and offer substantive claims finally unveiled themselves and took a seat amongst us. Some of our deepest convictions were fully exposed. How audacious. How tragic. The community that surrounded these burgeoning proclaimers negated that they had anything worth saying or listening to. And now the questions before our entire group were, "Will we continue to believe the lies we have internalized?" and "How does this influence our preaching?" And as a professor, I was challenged yet again by a feeling of failure and the relentless tasks of teaching and writing with contested voices and bodies as the starting point.

Faux Pioneering in the Ministries of Black Women

Preaching and listening to sermons is a learned and cultural act laden with assumptions. The woman who met me at the edge of the front pew measured that moment by her previous experiences of preaching. She had a framework in her mind. She helps name the space every preacher and listener negotiates. The preacher, even as she occupies her particular body and uses words within a particular space, is constantly in tension with received traditions of how a sermon takes shape and is performed and the look of the bodies that carry out its performance. The processes of listening and understanding are also shaped by these traditions.

Preaching assumes that those in a community give you authority to name and construct truth with them. The act assumes a place at the table and the validity of your voice. Tradition, the generally contested role of women in society and religion, and listener expectations continue to shape how women are and are not perceived as legitimate proclaimers. Although women have been preaching throughout time, points of friction remain around the presence of their bodies and acts of proclamation. Women who proclaim are often faced with conditions that mirror pioneering or the breaking of new ground. There are numerous old roots and thorns to work through. Even when these tensions are not overt, they remain subliminal and rumble beneath the surface.

When attending to the ministries and reception of black women who preach, we cannot detach the narratives of race, class, ability, and sexuality that accompany their bodies from their preaching practices. The limited confines we place on envisioning preaching and the legitimate proclaimer hearken back to a world where media, political machines, and economic structures still call into question black women's capabilities to name and define reality. This is the same world that creeps in and allows us to question a preacher's femininity, masculinity, and ability to construct meaningful words. "Sounding like a woman" has just as much to do with perceptions of one's ability to reason as it does with vocal pitch and intonation. And "sounding like a man" is seeded in the perception of authority being the antithesis of femininity, as Victorian ideals cast shadows on black womanhood. If a preacher strays too far to the left or right of a listener's center then she has not preached the mythical sermon or "black sermon" at all.

Black women continue to preach effectively even as they exist within the constant tension of pioneering and faux pioneering. The point of marvel without offense should be the choreography of this complex dance. How these proclaimers negotiate external expectations and demands while inventing and performing the sermon is something from which a spectrum of individuals can learn. We are constantly attempting to mediate expectations and retain some form of authenticity in preaching, while helping listeners connect with what is said. This dynamic requires a person to deploy creativity and know-how while navigating potential obstacles to her message, including how she is or is not perceived as a preacher.

Resetting the Rules of Engagement

As we look at the litany of hashtags, headlines, and fatalities that have bubbled up from the surface into plain view, people are not claiming themselves as outsiders or others. Instead, people are explicitly naming and giving witness to what happens when the world has declared them as outsiders, when they are not viewed as belonging or having a rightful seat at the table of full personhood. And most importantly, black women are naming the conditions and terms on which they will move about in the world—unequivocally black, woman, and human.

Toni Morrison, in her *The Origin of Others*, delineates how the category of *other* has been used in history and particularly in the literary arts. She argues that *other* as a category and *othering* as a practice are means of estrangement for one's own empowerment. It is a move that aligns with

introduction

power for the sake of solidifying belonging and is rarely used in benign terms for the sake of identifying distinctives in characteristics and identity alone.[3] The question to preaching and to those of us belonging to communities of faith is, "What then does this mean for our work?"

I posit first and foremost, those we have most excluded from the conversation, by deeming them as the *other* or *outsider*, must set the terms for our rules of engagement. If we do not privilege the lives and truth of the most vulnerable in our communities, then we cannot be faithful to the most fundamental work of preaching itself. Therefore, in these pages I am endeavoring in a process that revisits the rules for engaging the practice of preaching if we are committed to taking the lives and ministries of black women seriously. I will offer some distinct characteristics of preaching that emerge when beginning with the experiences, sermons, and tasks of black-preaching-women. Black women become the lens through which our collective paradigms of preaching and its instruction are revisited, reshaped, and broadened.

Interwoven within each chapter are brief sermon excerpts from preachers with some descriptive analysis of the content. These sections offer an opportunity to see the assumptions and arguments of the book at work, while hoping to subtly exclaim, "Black women preach!" The observations and arguments that I make are in conversation with thirty sermons by seven women. Through their sermons, these preachers graciously gave me windows into their preaching ministries, faith convictions, and work as those who proclaim. You will meet them as Barbara, Valerie, Sharon, Louise, Teresa, Patricia, and Vicki. My hope is to emphasize that the words we encounter are not just words, but the thoughts and ideas of these particular women as confessed before their communities of faith for the purpose of the community's ongoing faith development. Therefore, while I do not use their real names, they are named to recall this to our memory. The excerpts from their sermons by no means lay dormant on a page but once went forth as utterances that intersected with a community's deepest histories, thoughts, and beliefs. And these utterances somehow continue to leave imprints on the alchemy of those communities.

introduction

These clergy and their sermons fall into three major categories. The first category includes sermons by people who hold high teaching-preaching pastor positions within a congregational setting. The second category includes sermons by people who are associate pastors within a congregational setting and who preach at least seven times per year in that congregation. The third category includes sermons by itinerant preachers who preach in various locations at least six times per year. These preachers each have a minimum of five years of preaching experience, and their self-described denominational affiliations include United Methodist, African Methodist Episcopal, Presbyterian (PCUSA), Baptist (non-descriptive), Interfaith, and Pentecostal, while their primary home bases for ministry include the United States' eastern seaboard, southeast, and southwest. I do not offer long biographical sketches of these preachers, not because I deem them unimportant, but because I own that I have hunches and arguments at work, which I would like to interrogate against what is present in preaching on the ground. In short, this is not a full ethnographic study, nor is it intended to be an interrogation or critique of specific preachers. Yet the sermons can never be fully detached from the women that brought them to bear.

I am intentional here about my inclusion of sermons by women who may not have advanced training or formal education in Womanist, feminist, gendered, or theological studies, while not explicitly excluding women who do have such training. The major reasoning for this approach is to acknowledge that there is a different type of awareness that may or may not be present in the preaching task with such formalized training. The assumption of this work, which will be made clear, is that women with or without formal training in the aforementioned areas are engaging in a creative use of their wisdom, intellect, and faith convictions as they preach. Their creative wisdom is all the more meaningful when it is utilized in spaces that have not historically privileged the presence of black women in the role of preacher. It is meaningful because these women are preaching and people are listening. And in turn, they are overcoming what could be major obstacles to the reception of their message. In a similar manner, I have chosen to exclude women who have a nationally recognized platform in the form of a well-recognized television presence. National ministries targeting live and television audiences cater to a different speaker and listener relationship than those ministries that are based on an immediate live encounter in the same space.

The unpolished and polished packaging of the creative genius at work in the preaching of black women is precisely the beauty of their practice. This wise intuition is situated at the intersection of the preacher, the community, and the traditions in which she exists and interacts. Preaching necessitates both creativity and wisdom, while the preacher seeks a message that has implications for "right here and right now." For those often second-guessed and discredited in the call to construct meaningful speech for faith communities and the world writ large, developing homiletical wisdom and learning to trust one's judgment are pivotal in supporting the work of proclamation that sustains life—specifically one's own life and then the life of her community.

chapter 1

When Bodies and Unimaginative Practice Collide

A preacher's use of tradition has less to do with her acting and sounding like a man, sounding like a woman, giving away her voice, or acquiescing to power and more to do with reimagining expectations for her own purposes. Such a process of reimagining is undergirded and colored by the preacher's own ways of knowing—her voice. A preacher riffs off the expectations of preaching for the sake of her message, her process of constructing meaning, and preaching in her context. This riffing is the work of every preacher.

When a preacher uses a tradition for her own purposes in preaching, these are the moments in which she creatively invents without complete conformity. As one riffs without complete conformity and is allowed to do so, she most fully comes into her preaching voice in community. Her use of the tools at hand creates the opportunity to curate an alternative vision of preaching in the community. Preaching and the ability to make play on expectations become the mechanisms by which one comes into her preaching voice, reshapes communal understandings of preaching, and in its fullest expressions reshapes a community's frameworks of faith.

At minimum this reconstruction is one that expands confining assumptions about who is and who is not a legitimate proclaimer. At best this reconstruction shifts problematic ideologies that afforded such limitations to exist in the first place. Through preaching we are able to help a community fully embrace an otherwise minoritized body in its pulpit space. Preaching also opens opportunities for a community to interrogate its assumptions about who cannot create meaning with and on behalf of the community. Preaching holds the potential to shift the ways in which a community can "listen to a woman say it" and respond with "Yes!" as opposed to meeting a woman with silence or lack of affirmation while needing to hear a man say "it" before responding with a "Yes!"

Although the process of engaging a community's expectations for the sake of preaching is the work of every preacher in time, when black women undertake these actions their actions have a distinct outcome and texture. The location of black women in both their communities and the wider world places demands upon their voices in the work of overcoming obstacles to have their truth received. In preaching, black women have the task of deciding how they will or will not negotiate expectations about their abilities to speak and offer valid speech for the sake of the entire community. And as they make these negotiations, the preaching of black women has the possibility to reconstruct problematic ideologies as they call forward implicit assumptions related to the performativity, value, and place of black womanhood.

Black. Woman. Preacher.

The concurrent existence of black, woman, and preacher reflexively shapes black women's preaching practices. The experiences of being black, woman, and preacher simultaneously converge in the world of the-black-preaching-woman, establishing a particular persona. In addition, there are the expectations of the listener. In other words, the content and style of black women's preaching are extensions of both their social location and the high expectations of their preaching.

Social location and religious practices are not mutually exclusive entities in the lives of black women; they overlap with one another. Their overlap often relegates black women to an outsider-within position, not only in life at-large, but also in their communities of faith. If we are to engage the preaching of black women on its own terms, we cannot adequately do so without considering how their lived experiences are shaped by the intersections of race, class, sexuality, and gender. The experiences of present-day black women in North America are connected to a history that differentiates their experiences of racism from those of black men and their experiences of sexism from those of other women.

One aspect of black women's history in North America is the experience of being a captured—or *caged*—group for the social and economic gain of other individuals. The most recognizable aspects of this captivity are in the transatlantic slave trade. The less visible, but no less stigmatizing, aspects of being caged are the domestic servitude that followed the era of slavery and its ongoing mutations; their offspring yield income gaps, healthcare disparities, and higher death rates for these women in the twenty-first century. The realities of slavery and servitude are portraits of the social, and conversely economic, categories to which others have assigned black women based on race and gender. Indeed, both institutions were concrete realities and continue to loom as metaphors for the system of social control that still mitigate black women's struggles for social equality.[1] Black women's assigned social locations have often led to their erasure, invisibility, and a controlled narrative surrounding the significance of their presence in history.[2]

The limited power given to black women to record and document their own *herstory* perpetuates ideologies about them as opposed to promoting their writing and inscribing their own identities. We see this limited power in the sparse historical documents of black women's preaching and sermons that predate the twentieth century.[3] The result is the perpetuation of descriptors placed upon black women, or none at all, as opposed to descriptions and documentation of the lives of black women written by black women. Historically, black women, as both *black* and *woman*, remain(ed) as outsiders-within[4] movements that have been classified as either black or woman, as their voices are not directly engaged in conversations that pertain to their existence. Our understandings of preaching are not excluded from this critique, yet these understandings are further shaped by the gendered dynamics in communities of faith.

chapter 1

As communities of faith adopt theological ideas and explications of suffering from early Christian traditions, they simultaneously solidify troublesome gender relations and the injustices perpetuated by such understandings of gender and power. The early Christian traditions rely on themes of male dominance, righteousness versus unrighteousness, and sanctified suffering. The acceptance and adoption of theological ideals and explications of suffering inherent in the Christian tradition have yet to be *fully* interrogated by faith communities on the ground under the guise of liberation and its implications on the lives and status of black women. This lack of robust interrogation of the tradition by some faith communities results in ongoing gendered power imbalances within these same communities. Many churches continue to relegate the position of black women to a subordinate status.

The symptomatic issues of the intra-group tension between black women and men are demonstrated through the struggles of women who preach, pastor, serve, and attend predominantly black Protestant churches in the United States.[5] Women account for the largest base in black church congregations yet are disproportionately represented in roles of pastoral leadership. While women are often excluded from positions of primary leadership along with ministries of teaching and preaching at senior levels, women are "allowed" to pursue the positions of administrative assistants, teachers of children and of some adult Sunday school classes, and leaders of women's auxiliaries; they are also expected to fully support if not undergird the financial vitality of the churches. Both men and women restrict the participation of women within churches, yet their participation is vital within these churches for the institution's flourishing and continued existence.

These politics of power have led to conceptualizing the black preacher as black and male in rather robust narratives and images. The robust depiction of the black preacher as specifically male sharply contrasts with an underdeveloped, if not lacking, image of the-black-preaching-woman. This underdeveloped image of the-black-preaching-woman leads to underdeveloped understandings of black women's preaching ministries. Evidence of these underdeveloped aspects of both the-black-preaching-woman and her preaching is found within their absorption into conversations about black and women's preaching traditions via limited distinction from their preaching peers in a way that accounts for their experiences as both black and woman.⁶ The-black-preaching-woman becomes invisible within discourses about black preaching, as often these discourses have focused historically on black men; likewise, the-black-preaching-woman becomes invisible within discourses about women's preaching, as these discourses have focused historically on white women. All the women are white; all the preachers are men.⁷

It is important to say a word here to discourage monolithic narratives about what it means to be a black-preaching-woman. Even as race, class, and gender are common contributing factors in the lives of black women, thus requiring the categories of black and woman to be interrogated more fully, we cannot assume a common experience amongst black women. All black women do not respond to and experience the meeting of race, sexuality, class, and gender in the same manner.⁸ There are a variety of black women's experiences, and with these different experiences comes different forms of outsider-within privileges. For instance, the distinctives between women from different socioeconomic backgrounds is palpable. The ongoing iterations of race, class, and gendered discrimination in the lives of black women, as opposed to symmetry in experience, allow us to retain social location as an important starting point in understanding their lives, religious practices, and preaching.

Every black woman does not struggle with trusting her judgment or preaching voice. But to be sure, we live in a world that has violently contested the presence of black women's voices and bodies. These contestations are not disconnected from racist, sexist, and classist frameworks. And these frameworks are connected to the invisibility and erasure of a complex portrait of black-preaching-women, especially within communities of faith.

The Limits and Dangers of Unimaginative Practice

When preaching and its hopes are conflated with the presence or absence of a particular body, that body inherently restricts the possibility of preaching. Preaching becomes an unimaginative practice. The fields in which proclamation may occur are now limited, narrowed, and confined. This mirrored illusion of preaching that is perpetuated by communal rigidity closes preaching off from its own possibilities—the free-expression, unlimited, and unrestrained encounter of sacred-in-breaking. The spirit of God that enables preaching through her free will has now been confined to a community's terms and conditions.

These expectations of preaching have undermined the very rationale of preaching and have replaced it with bodily productions. The oxygen that gave preaching its very purpose and hopes is restricted. And the result is death unto preaching itself, as it permeates into a synthetic image and illusion of itself. And concretely, in this same way historically, the expectation of a particular and preferred type of masculinity in bodily productions of preaching has pushed preaching into a practice of production and imitation. Preaching has been replaced by the politics of the pulpit as a gendered space,[9] and it is this space that regulates the practice of preaching more than the hope of preaching itself.

As opposed to existing as a practice that generates fully new possibilities, the ephemeral scaffolding of preaching has closed preaching off from its own possibilities. In turn, this narrowed scope collides with the bodies that are most marginalized, are least valued, or are desired invisible by the community. This collision happens as these bodies listen to what is offered through preaching and especially when they themselves attempt to preach.

The Collision of Unimaginative Practice with Real Bodies

The push-and-pull experienced by black women who preach is a distinct result of unimaginative practice and bodies others desire to be invisible. There are organizing principles (scaffolding) that have established what *black preaching* is and, in return, what the "black sermon" looks and sounds like. These organizing principles have been proliferated within and outside communities of faith. This ephemeral scaffolding is influenced by wider cultural myths about black preaching that do not escape racist stereotypes of black performance, which will be discussed further in chapter 2. The established image of the black preacher continues to advance an understanding and practice of preaching in the flesh, and in this regard it continues to reinforce these same established images and practices of black preaching. Depictions of the black male as preacher and the safeguarding of male privilege within black churches regulate the framework of preaching. The framework creates a largely unvaried understanding of black preaching within its various contexts of depiction, while it continues alongside the larger ongoing practice of preaching.[10] Black women's preaching practices are often in juxtaposition to the established image of the black preacher, which is overwhelmingly associated with a black male and a particular performance of masculinity.[11]

The image of the black preacher presents a male with rhetorical prowess, a voice of thunder, and the ability to move the community to ecstasy highs while weaving together the life of the text and life in the world.[12] Similarly, black preaching is etched as holding in tension the experience of the community with an all-powerful God; it is emotive, keeping with a particular rhythm and cadence, and includes aspects of celebration that intentionally bring the heart, body, and mind together in the preaching moment. Whether individuals actively resist or adopt this practice of preaching, it functions as a narrative that links black preaching to a particular performance of masculinity in pulpit space and rhetoric. Thus, it links the practice of preaching to masculinity, privileging the bodily productions of a particular type of a heterosexual black cisgender male over the hopes of an encounter with proclamation.

There has not been "one conductor" or "wizard" behind the image's perpetuation; to the contrary, the image has been "collectively orchestrated" by various facets of history.[13] Black women also engage and participate in this understanding when they preach, both by force and choice. Women, who preach within these traditions, constantly imagine and invent their sermons in conversation with and in juxtaposition to the tradition and its inherent power in a community; this requires both creativity and ingenuity[14] for the sake of (re)imagining both the sermon and preaching. The result is a spectrum of approaches to preaching by black women, who are aware of the elusive yet overt parameters that mark "legitimate" preaching.

When expectations centered on performances of masculinity determine what is and is not valid preaching, these expectations render black women as bodies of difference or bodies desired to be unseen in the pulpit (desired invisible). Black women are displaced from the pulpit and their citizenship status within the community is that of outsider. As these women continue to participate within these communities and around these understandings of preaching, they are inextricably a part of a system.

However, as they are embedded within the structures of these communal expectations, they also creatively engage the power postulated by the tradition and its guardians. Their preaching is the tactical expression of their own creativity and ingenuity.[15] Black preaching women riff off of the expectations of preaching and its ephemeral scaffolding, for the sake of the hope and ethics preaching espouses—a word from God that fosters life abundant. As they do this, preaching becomes the means by which synthetic practices of preaching are disrupted in both more hushed and resounding ways; in turn, the community generates new possibilities and means of understanding preaching as its members are able to say, "This 'too' is preaching!"[16]

Womanist practical theologians and homileticians intentionally work to name the resounding ways of disrupting synthetic faith practices that are overwhelmingly male preferential. Evelyn Parker notes that one of the concerns germane to womanist practical theology is the consideration for how "pastoral and ecclesial praxis bring about life-giving ministries for the flourishing of black women and girls, the black community, and the entire world."[17] To these ends, homiletician Teresa Fry Brown describes black women's preaching as a practice that can directly confront injustices and transform religious spaces and traditions. She specifically describes black women's preaching as having the potential to "renovate sorrow's kitchen" (her metaphor for the black church) through using the "tools of renovation."[18] The tools of renovation involve the preacher using "a fresh reading of the text" and "relentlessly engaging injustices," as she articulates her standard of justice and carves out her own space.[19] Fry Brown makes clear that the presence of a black woman in the pulpit creates new visions for both the image of preacher and the image of justice; and it is equally clear that the work of the womanist preacher does not stop at pulpit presence. In a similar trajectory, Donna E. Allen pushes for a *trans-rationale* understanding of womanist preaching, which explicitly attends to the linguistic, ethical, and embodied dimensions of liberationist preaching by black women.[20] The emphasis in these intentional modes of disruption is the assumption that black women have the capacity to act and their actions have moral dimensions that affect their lives and the lives of their communities.

What follows builds upon these assumptions about the presence and experiences of black women as they intersect with pulpit spaces, while underscoring the more hushed but no less morally significant iterations of these encounters. Everyday women put their real bodies and expressions in contact with unimaginative and restrictive worship spaces; in their preaching we often witness fragments of equity and justice push through and sneak past the very structures that seek to render violence and injustice in their lives.[21] As preachers better understand these working tools and tactics, they can make more strategic use of them for the sake of God's justice in the community and world.[22] In short, framing preaching within the practice of ingenuity helps the preacher make greater use of the power to which she has access already.[23]

An Act of Constrained Invention

Preaching is the act of invention. This act of invention requires pulling together pieces for something that does not yet exist—that is, the sermon. Every sermon begins with having "nothing yet" to preach. To develop a sermon requires weaving together loose edges until something new comes forth.[24] Preaching is an imaginative work. This work engages a very aesthetic process of pursuing one's best hunches and seeking rhythmic alignment among the ancient worlds of sacred texts, the contemporary world, and the preacher's own intuition. Often the process is one of creating alignment where it does not readily exist. This is the imagination at work in preaching—finding similarities alongside dissimilarities for the sake of precision in message.[25] The imagination through preaching forges the contours of an invention that is more than the sum of its parts. The preacher has to imagine words into being where they do not yet exist.[26] Her imagining is inextricably connected to a community's ability to imagine. For the community has its own imaginings of the preacher, the sermon, and proclamation in its context.

In this creative process the one who preaches is in constant conversation with a tradition, expectations, and hopes as they are both named and unnamed within a community. These named and unnamed realities include the presumed limitations of what preaching is and is not. For example, a sermon is in conversation with a community's standards related to sermon length, timing, appropriate content, and determinations about how political and pastoral a message should be, about how overtly or subtly naming God and the presence of God is attended to in the message, and even how the preacher is personified in their contexts. The content, shape, and form of preaching are based upon blueprints constructed by a community.

Therefore, the aim here is to offer ways for us to consider expanding preaching as a practice, as we attend to its hopes even as we often engage a community's confining expectations of a sermon. I place these expectations in conversation with what we know and understand about preaching, homiletic theory, and preaching traditions, particularly black and women's preaching traditions. Turning to the sermon and its development becomes a means of broadening both our hopes and processes of preaching, particularly when considering individuals who preach from a minoritized place within a community. A sermon's content and structure are parts of the scaffolding that facilitate the preaching moment, the preacher's ability to overcome obstacles to their message, and the possibility of reshaping communal understandings. My intention is not to say what preaching cannot be, as much as it is to say *what more preaching might actually be and do.*

The following chapter explains ingenuity as a framing for a theology and practice of preaching that emerges from the preaching ministries of black women. Ingenuity broadens understandings of the pulpit and preaching within a community; and at best, it espouses a sacred-in-breaking that reorients our ways of thinking, being, and doing for the sake of life at hand. Proclamation for black women is a generative disruption supported by creativity.

Chapters 3, 4, 5, and 6 attend to the shape of sermon development and design that builds upon ingenuity. These chapters mirror each other in format and are divided into four major sections with distinct tones. Each chapter is framed within an aspect of what listeners often expect in preaching, and then considers how those expectations intersect with the personhood of black women. The second section of these chapters analyzes how those expectations appear in the sermons of black women as they are navigated by preachers. The third section names how black women make creative use of the expectations under consideration. And, the final chapter section explores what this all might mean for sermon development as a whole, including practical helps for every preacher.

With this framework, chapter 3 explores how a preacher engages everyday life as a resource for message development. Engaging the experiences of black women as primary resources for preaching recovers narratives that are often ignored. A preacher's ability to effectively engage life in this manner often requires a subtle and seamless weaving of new narratives and familiar narratives.

Chapter 4 names the use of scripture for preaching as a type of play and interplay in the movement between ancient and contemporary worlds, while retaining both life and scripture as sacred texts in preaching. Preaching as an outsider necessitates one being astute in knowing when and how to use caution or take liberties in interpretive decisions.

Chapter 5 attends to how preaching within a framework of ingenuity relies on a communally-assertive preaching authority. These types of messages possess contemporary veracity, while they show forth immediate implications for the survival and thriving of a community. Such an approach to shaping a message for preaching disrupts false binaries between authoritative and communal approaches to preaching.

chapter 1

    Sermons undergirded with contemporary veracity and authority assume God is near and present in the everyday world. They depend on the preacher's ability to recast the story of faith. Sacred storytelling through preaching is the focus of chapter 6, and requires the nuanced grounding of faith claims in their ordinary implications for both the individual and the community as they exist in the wider world.

    In the final chapter, I share the ways in which particularity shapes every preaching ministry. And in turn, learning from a variety of preaching ministries is the only way preachers cultivate the wisdom and ingenuity necessary for preaching in their specific context.

chapter 2
Ingenuity for the Sake of Proclamation

Just as a bridge or road sign points in a particular direction, the ongoing work of preaching as it occurs within a community leads us along a path indicating what preaching should entail. This historical path consists of road signs that point in a particular direction in terms of what is fitting or even "good" preaching. These blueprints are formulated against the backdrop of preaching both as it takes place at a very particular moment in a very particular community and as it has occurred over time.[1] For instance Mary Magdalene's announcement of the gospel via the sermon that names Jesus's resurrection is not disconnected from the preaching of Prathia Hall, Malcolm X, T. D. Jakes, Joel Olsteen, Otis Moss Jr., Gina Stewart, and the many unnamed. Every one of these proclaimers in their various iterations of preaching is connected to a tradition across time and space. There is a wide tradition of preaching that intersects with the practices of preaching at any given point in time. Therefore, as preaching has the ability to take on new flesh within a community, every preacher and community stands in conversation—and often times in tension—with a tradition beyond herself and the community.

The tension between this tethering of history and the not-yet existent in imagining is what makes for the possibilities and limits of preaching, especially for those who preach as outsiders. The effective preacher finds ways to be in conversation with and utilize assumptions about preaching while overlaying her own intonation, pitch, and coloring to the task. The one who proclaims effectively uses the road sign as just that—a road sign—as she engages her own wisdom, creativity, and imaginings for the sake of the community. Indeed, this is the beautiful balancing act and skillful pursuit of every preacher. She makes use of tradition for the sake of the community for which she speaks but also for the community's hopes about what preaching renders possible. Namely, preaching renders possible a not-yet-existent, though somewhat known, encounter with the sacred.

The hope in preaching is the possibility of our being interlopers on sacred utterances, which only emerge because God chooses to self-reveal in our midst. Preaching is a practice that depends and hopes upon sacred-in-breaking, while it is also tethered to our human capacity to imagine and reimagine its limits and possibilities. As sacred reverberations occur in our midst, they push us to reimagine the possibilities of life together and even the possibilities (and contours) of preaching (and the preacher). When something more than the compilation of words, images, ideas, and their structures pushes through and past the sermon, the community recognizes it as proclamation or as truth proclaimed.

Preaching as a Communally Defined Practice

Our understanding of preaching is derived in community and by the community. The collective defines what is and what is not a valid expression of preaching in its midst and sets boundaries on preaching based on an inherited and often reproduced experience of preaching. The aural-oral tradition of call and response in some black preaching traditions offers us a glimpse of a community setting the boundaries and limits of preaching. In the preaching moment a listener may verbally offer the following responses: "That's preaching!" "Preach!" "Yea, that's good," or "Take your time." These call outs of affirmation not only urge the preacher to forge ahead in her immediate practice of preaching but also somehow act as an indicator of what preaching should be, how it should function, and its shape within the community. Similarly, "Be careful!" "Help him, Lord!" or the eerie presence of silence where one would hope for an audible response might be the setting of another boundary and limit, as listeners express that the right-fitting and desired scaffolding is absent. In this instance, the community withdraws its validation from what is right preaching; in other words, "That's not preaching."

As the community sets the parameters of preaching in its midst based on past experiences, it also intentionally or unknowingly defines the future and continual practice of preaching in its midst. The body is far from incidental in the process of marking a discrete moment of preaching as valid. Preaching is carried out by flesh and lands upon flesh. Therefore, we cannot discard the body as a vehicle, nor its influence, in carrying forth the memory of preaching in a community. The boundaries and expectation of preaching within a community are very much dictated, formed, and understood by the way preaching is carried forth through the body and how preaching encounters the body.

When we limit preaching to the embodiment of its practice, as opposed to the hoped-for thing preaching makes way for—namely, proclamation—the body no longer becomes a medium for preaching. Instead the body is a perceived limitation to preaching; this perception of the body as a limitation is acutely true when particular individuals are valued more or less because of the bodies they inhabit. For instance, women are often told, "Good speech," as opposed to, "Good sermon." Differently-abled individuals may not be readily visualized as "preachers." Here the presence of a body is only valued based on what it can and cannot produce. Namely, "Does one preach like these other bodies?" If the answer is yes, then "that's preaching." If the answer is no, then "that's not preaching." In these scenarios it is no longer the rationale or ethic of preaching that drives its practice; the ability to mimic and imitate the history of preaching as experienced drives the practice forward.[2] And here is where we potentially close off preaching and the possibilities of sacred-in-breaking through the very continual and ongoing practice of preaching itself. Yet some determine ways to work with expectations for their own purposes.

chapter 2

Proclamation as a Marking Experience

Proclamation is an evocative occasion and its presence makes an inscription upon that which it encounters. Proclamation renders marks upon our existence in both describable and indescribable ways; it possesses a type of elusive yet qualitative essence. If we were to consider moments in which proclamation occurs, be it in the form of words, deeds, or expressions, we might describe it as something affirmed and recognizable by those gathered.

These utterances, which are often fleeting experiences, are significantly meaningful to an individual or the collective—often both. When we encounter proclamation or it encounters us, we affirm that *something* meaningful has occurred. One's ability to ascribe meaning and significance to an encounter is held within and shaped by her wider communal contexts. Similarly, if a community deems something as worthy of its attention and a legitimate marker of its existence, personal buy-in from individuals is a predetermining factor for establishing collective import. When experienced, proclamation is an encounter meaningful enough to be accepted as valid or true in as far as it aligns with what one affirms, wishes to affirm, or is synergistic with lived experience.

And in its noteworthiness, proclamation reconfigures borders and boundaries in the lives of individuals and their communities based on new or realigned understandings. This reconfiguration may take place in the form of affirming existing beliefs and experiences and encouraging practices that further shape the continuation of those beliefs and experiences. Or this reconfiguration may occur as pushing the community and individuals into new futures of their beliefs and practices based on reshaped or expanded understandings. In these instances proclamation does not simply affirm but pushes and expands.

For communities of faith, proclamation possesses the nature of something more—namely, the ripples of sacred-in-breaking. In the most traditional sense it is named as word of God when recognized. The hope in preaching is not simply the mechanics of words, symbols, structures, form, proper images, and analogies. The hope in preaching is the process of making way for and limiting obstacles to the opportunity for proclamation to occur. This moment of proclamation may take the form of robust vibrations or simple ripples that realign or (re)imprint in the most subtle of ways. Whether it is a grandiose appearance or a hushed voice, proclamation is the moment in which the mundane has made way for what is holy, sacred, and counted as true to appear in the midst of those gathered. The community recognizes or bears witness to this moment when it occurs. Proclamation has the characteristics of that which rings true and clear, and while it is the anticipated moment in preaching, it is not guaranteed in preaching.

Proclamation and Preaching

Just as the community recognizes expressions that ring as truth in its midst, its histories also shape the recognition of this truth. Based on past occurrences, we recognize the signaling toward proclamation. There are ways in which we intuit that something significant is happening or occurring; there is often a relationship to how we experience a present encounter of proclamation and past moments of such experiences. Our body, mind, and heart react to that which bears witness to our deepest places of knowing, and we remember this bodily knowing when we encounter such a witness once again. The moment may be perceived as an answer to a concern or question, accepted as affirmation of an inclination or hoped-for thing, an echoing backward or forward to conversations and a way of knowing, and even a physical sensation that hits the hallows of our being. When proclamation happens the entirety of our being recognizes its presence as it engages the multitude of our intelligences, including our physical, cognitive, emotional, and spiritual ways of knowing.

While there may be individual and physiological signals toward proclamation we are also aware of the mediums of proclamation in our midst. Though we cannot guarantee how, when, or the site of proclamation, we are familiar with what signals toward proclamation and the scaffolding that makes way for it. In communities of faith, preaching signals toward proclamation. Preaching, therefore, can be considered the scaffolding that helps support proclamation.

The acceptance and recognition of preaching as scaffolding for proclamation, or that which makes way for proclamation, are shaped by past experiences of preaching and its practice in the community. Over time communities of faith develop an association not only between proclamation and preaching but also between the how and what of preaching as it makes may for proclamation. Preaching that makes way for proclamation is an understanding defined and derived from the ways a community has come to understand what preaching "ought and should do" in order to make way for sacred-in-breaking.

The Black Preacher as a Ghostly Image

Black and male are the immediate images and meters that measure the rhetorical performance of the black sermon, even if merely at the subconscious level. The legitimate practices and function of the preacher within the context of black religious life have influenced images of the black preacher, as well as the descriptive and prescriptive caricatures, judgments, and assumptions of his skeptics and genuine supporters.[3] As stated in the previous chapter, images of the black preacher have negative and positive characteristics based on a skewed history, racist stereotypes, and the actions of preachers themselves. And, over time, the "images" have converged into one predominate "image" that is unequivocally black and male. Beyond pulpits and pews, we encounter "real and imagined"[4] constructions of this preacher in the bodies and narratives of actual preachers, in American literature, as well as in contemporary media and artistic expressions.

As the slave preacher and more prominent public figures influence our conceptualization of the black preacher, American literature leads us most keenly into the image of the black preacher as a cultural product described and re-signified through cultural productions. Literature captures the bodily performance of the black preacher and the content of the black sermon. Writers often caricature the preacher as a black man with rhetorical prowess, a voice of thunder, and an unmet imagination that weaves the biblical text with the realities of lived black experience. In the preface to *God's Trombones: Seven Negro Sermons in Verse*, James Weldon

Johnson describes the black preacher as "above all an orator" who has the ability to move congregations to "ecstasy by the rhythmic intoning of sheer incoherencies," while using the modulation of his voice to perform poetic language.[5] In his work, Johnson portrays the poetic language and performance of the black preacher and sermon in seven poems.

And, just as Johnson emulates the black preacher in poetry, black women write about the images of the black preacher in literary fiction. Black women's fiction has been a place for women to explore their experiences of black womanhood in North America, as well as a means to disclose facts in fiction. The literature encapsulates the history of black preaching traditions, while it also reveals the characteristics used to describe black preaching in its caricatures and homiletics to date.

For instance, in 1934, Zora Neale Hurston reproduced the historical image of the preacher in *Jonah's Gourd Vine*, a novel that was based on her own contemporary experiences.[6] Hurston incorporates her field notes of a country preacher into the depiction of a final sermon given by the novel's protagonist, John Buddy Pearson. John's sermon is entitled "The Wounds of Jesus" and is based on Isaiah 53.[7] In it, Hurston inscribes aspects of slow delivery, celebration, imaginative language, intonation, rhythm, whooping, and musicality.[8]

Hurston links the musicality in John's sermon with a song he leads the congregation in just prior to preaching.[9] John Buddy and his preaching are characterized as igniting the congregation while the congregation is described in turn as "bearing up" almost continuously throughout the sermon.[10] Hurston's description parallels Johnson's description of the black preacher moving the congregation to "ecstasy." She describes John beginning his sermon in a "clear, calm voice,"[11] followed by hesitation, and eventually moving to rhythmic celebration.

Hurston consistently uses grammatical constructions of dashes to demonstrate aspects of slow delivery and voice modulation in the progression of John's sermon. For example, in one instance, John says: "I can see-eeee-ee De Mountains fall to their rocky knees when he cried."[12] Hurston also uses grammatical constructions to portray the rhythmic nature and verbal intonation of preaching:

> When you are alone to yourself
> When yo' heart is burnt with fire, ha!
> When de blood is lopin' thru yo' veins
> Like de iron monasters (monsters) on de rail
> Look into dat upper chamber, ha!
> We notice at de supper table
> As He gazed upon His Friends, ha!
> His eyes flowin' wid tears, ha! He said
> My soul is exceedingly sorrowful unto death, ha!
> For this night, ha!
> One of you shall betray me, ha![13]

Here, Hurston's use of short phrases and "ha!" signifies hard pauses in the sermon's height of emotive celebration, which is rooted in the death, burial, and resurrection of Jesus. The reader can almost hear John preaching. Just as Johnson does in his own text, Hurston portrays the codified image of the black preacher, based on historical and contemporary experiences of the black male. Ironically, Hurston's contemporary descriptors remain continuous with our present-day descriptions of black preaching, even as the bodies may not be named as overtly male in current preaching literature.

As the image of the black preacher and the black sermon is predominantly caricatured as black and male, when and where the-black-preaching-woman occurs in literature are striking. Roxanne Mountford describes the American Protestant pulpit as a male-dominated rhetorical space that has excluded and considered female bodies as weaker and inferior.[14] The embodiment of maleness and masculinity has rendered control over pulpit spaces. Mountford notes that when women are characterized as preachers in American literature they most often appear preaching "outside" of the pulpit space.[15] This characterization is also found right in the middle of black women's literature.

In contrast to John Buddy, another preacher prototype appears in Hurston's *Their Eyes Were Watching God*. The reader is only introduced to her as Nanny; she is the grandmother of the protagonist Janie Crawford. Nanny overtly says, "Ah wanted to preach a great sermon about colored women sitting on high, but there wasn't no pulpit for me."[16] Through

Nanny's words Hurston sheds light on both the male-oriented pulpit and the place of black women in society. While the pulpit has eluded Nanny and her sermon about the lives, strength, and God of black women, Baby Suggs, holy, in Toni Morrison's *Beloved*, creates a pulpit where one does not exist. Baby Suggs's platform is often a "huge-flat-rock."[17] And from this pulpit she invites the women to cry, the men to dance, and the children to laugh. She denounces the divide between the bodily and spiritual for the sake of proclamation that attends to the life of her community. For Baby Suggs, holy, is the classic black woman itinerant, who takes an audience where her spirit goes and with whomever's heart is open, be it at the kitchen table, a prayer meeting, or wide-open meadow. In these kinds of depictions of preaching, the male's control as orator and author of "sanctioned pulpit" speech is exemplified, providing commentary on a world in which a woman's place is outside the pulpit. However, the lives and stories of black women are not lost on these pulpit-less proclaimers, but they are the substance of their sermons. The lived wisdom of black women reshapes the work of these pulpit-less preaching women.

Following the present-day narratives of historical descriptions and literature, the black preacher is regularly cast as black and male in television, film, and theatre, including serious drama and comedic satires. In the 1985 film production of Alice Walker's *The Color Purple*, Shug Avery's father, the local preacher, sits in the center of a predominantly female congregation. The title of the 1996 film "The Preacher's Wife" inherently assumes and underscores that the preacher is male. We see similar occurrences in Tyler Perry's production of screenplays and movies, such as in "I Can Do Bad All By Myself" (2009); here, the preacher has a voice of thunder and a hum (and oftentimes a whoop), and his strong presence is unequivocally male. The juxtaposition of the debuts of two reality television series in 2013—*The Sisterhood* and *Preachers of L.A.*—reflects the ongoing cultural narratives about black preachers, women, and men. Both casts were predominately black. *Preachers of L.A.* portrays a cast of men who are preachers and are supported by their wives and partners, known as the "first ladies." The series *The Sisterhood* puts the first ladies in full view, as they fulfill leading and supporting roles but are not preachers. A rare depiction of the black preacher and pastor as woman appears in the 2003 film "Deliver Us from Eva." However, the character of pastor appears only briefly, standing *outside* of the church to greet the members of the congregation. Not a single scene depicts her preaching amongst the congregation. Thus, although the image of the black preacher is rooted in historical narratives and practice, contemporary cultural vehicles continue to disseminate the image.

The image of the black preacher remains a ghostly figure in the preaching ministries of black women. This historical ghost is perpetuated by gendered politics within and outside of black Christian communities, real preaching bodies, and cultural productions. The image has been narrowly contrived as a black male with rhetorical prowess, who has the ability to perform what is recognized as the black sermon. The image of the black preacher is elusive at times but not extinct. The image lingers and influences the expectations of what it means to be black and a preacher, regardless of whether the image is actively adopted, resisted, or acknowledged within a particular community.

Black women are competing with an established image when they preach; the ideal image, in its maleness, is inherently other than who black women are. Thus, black women are potentially still viewed outside the category of preacher. As a result, they negotiate a space for themselves and their voices across various contexts of ministry. This specific outside status of black women who preach creates experiences that are different from their preaching contemporaries.

A Practice That Opens and Generatively Disrupts

"I practice it because I think it's an art, but I ain't doing it." —Rev. Barb

These are the words that Roxanne Mountford ascribes as coming from Rev. Barb in her work *The Gendered Pulpit*. Reverend Barb is a black woman who preaches in a predominately black context and in a church that openly struggled with her position and hiring as pastor to the point that a small contingent of members threatened to leave at her appointment. While recalling hearing black preaching and particularly black men preaching on the tv and radio, she names the limits of her engagement with those tropes of the tradition, specifically whooping. Yet, Mountford offers a descriptive of Rev. Barb preaching during a Sunday morning worship service. Mountford names, appropriately or not, this preacher's work as an engendering of the black jeremiad.[18] The performance is similar to the ghostly image of the black preacher we have encountered already.

Mountford describes how the sermon built from a quiet voice to a near crescendo after Rev. Barb lead the congregation in song:

> The sermon was built on a series of stories designed to illustrate her point. She preached the first part in her quiet, alto voice, talking in a matter-of-fact tone, behind the pulpit. . . . But as she preached, she became more animated, her voice speeding up and slowing down to emphasize points. . . . Fifteen minutes into the sermon she abandoned the manuscript and began to walk—first out from behind the pulpit, then in front of the pulpit, then slowly down the center aisle. . . . She ended the sermon at the high emotional pitch right in the center of the congregation, and then asked "The doors of the church are wide open. Who will join the church today? Is there one?"[19]

The description of Rev. Barb's preaching contains hallmarks of the generally accepted narrative of black preaching practices. She powerfully shifts from a quieter voice to build up to a more direct speech. There is the presence of rhythm, cadence, and intonation for emphasis. Her voice demonstrates a "high emotional pitch," while her body joining the congregation in its center is indication of her using a form of celebration to close and end the sermon. Her celebration culminates as she extends an invitation to discipleship. In a follow-up interview with Mountford, Rev. Barb expressed an understanding of the expectation and pressure for her to be "the black preacher" while at the same time saying, "Yeah, I listen to them [black preaching men] on the radio and they just be doing it [hoot/whoop], and *I practice it* because I think it's an art, *but I ain't doing it.*"[20] Here, Rev. Barb acknowledges the tradition and, to some degree, embodies and practices it while also acknowledging her boundaries and the extent to which she will engage it.

Reverend Barb is keenly aware of black preaching traditions as they are performed within and alongside a particular performance of masculinity. And in the excerpt above, she utilizes aspects of its practice in her own preaching. However, she states that there are limitations on the degree to which she incorporates the understood traditional practice in her preaching, specifically in terms of the "hoot/whoop." She is able to speak the language and perform the art in a way that is understood and accepted by those listening. At the same time, her decision to style on the tradition makes use of the power it wields within the community in very different ways (*creative tactics*) than those she listens to on the radio. Most plausibly, the preacher's ability to use her creative wit and know-how in and for preaching is part and parcel to establishing herself as a preacher and pastor within a context that is resistant to her presence. Her use of preaching creates room for her body and voice. The preacher uses the traditional practice and expectation of black preaching for her own purposes.

Imitating, Mimicking, and Preaching

To an extent all preaching—and every beginning preacher—has its genesis in imitation. By the word *imitation*, I mean the act of a preacher mimicking the process they seek to perform and carry out, as they have experienced it. We only know what preaching is because of our exposure to preaching in community or from a distance, including both its best and worst practices alongside its myths and stereotypes. Because preaching is a communally defined and accountable process, those who preach render their rhetoric and performance out of the ways by which specific traditions or communities conceive valid preaching.

In addition to preaching being a practice that is learned through imitation and mimicking, individual preachers often imitate and mimic those with whom they find resonance in preaching. Preachers find their way into their preaching voice as they imitate preachers either who are admired in their tradition or whom they personally favor. This process of finding voice through others is a natural process of the journey of the preacher. However, there are limits to imitation and mimicking. This is particularly true for those who are minoritized in the preaching space, such as women, people who identify as LGBTQIA+, those with disabilities, and others who may perform outside of a community's preacher prototype. Creating one's preaching voice and moving toward authenticity are difficult when models that may have affinity with your evolving voice are not present.[21]

However, when the standard within a community's expectation of preaching stops at the replication of a particular style of performance, as opposed to living into preaching's exponential iterations, mimicking and imitation become mechanisms that contribute to closing preaching off from its purposes; and in turn, mimicking and imitation close a community off from the possibilities and hopes of preaching in its midst. There is an inherent difference between mimicking and imitating preaching styles to their ultimate ends and creatively riffing off and making use of an existent tradition and style as one finds their own voice.

Communal Choreography and Sacred Vibrations

Every preacher riffs on preaching expectations for the hope of naming something significantly meaningful for their community. Those who are particularly minoritized may use preaching expectations more intentionally and with more mindfulness, as they engage in a distinct creativity for the sake of what preaching demands of them in their contexts. When a preacher creatively makes use of tradition, they engage such tactics for the purpose of gaining a listening while overcoming obstacles in the reception of their message. Obstacles may range from "You don't look or sound like a preacher" to resistance to the proposal of an alternative faith narrative that potentially shifts communal outlooks on faith and the world.

Preaching is a creative process that exists within the playing fields of traditions. And ingenuity makes use of those playing fields, not just for the sake of preaching, but also for what preaching makes possible. Christian preaching traditions await and anticipate sacred vibrations breaking into our midst. This sacred-in-breaking is what draws us back to spaces of worship with a disposition of listening intently. These holy echoes move in and out of proximity to our awareness. Sometimes we recognize them and their call on our attention immediately. At other times we connect random dots over time among different conversations, thoughts, and moments of reflection. These are the characteristics of proclamation—fleeting, not always fully describable—but we know when it has encountered us and when we have encountered it. At such meeting places, we offer a resounding or more hushed affirmation of its presence in our midst—*Amen*.

However, a complex dance occurs between the *hopes* of offering up an *Amen*—a tradition we perceive to have made that *Amen* possible—and the bodies that are not allowed to move in and out of pulpit spaces. The parties of the dance are often reduced to the mechanics of rigid choreography, as opposed to allowing the music that sets the rhythm of the choreography to inspire the dance. The result is choreography (preaching) out of sync with the music of its inspiration (proclamation). Inspiration is traded for one's confidence in rigid movement (unimaginative practice) that does not fit *every* body attempting its sequence (the outsider). As a result, bodies are hurled in and out of the spiral of rigidity. We ignore, to the demise of many, the possibility of trusted choreography joining inspiration for the sake of a more creative dance that makes space for *every* body. In spite of the threats of rigidity, there are moments when unexpected things happen. People make use of choreography with a play on its past while pushing its present, and somehow inspiration breaks through. In this appearance, we are reminded of the authentic hopes of the dance once again.

Our hope in preaching is not replicating fixed patterns. Instead, our hope is to exchange fixed patterns for that which makes space for the vibrant possibilities of sacred-in-breaking in our midst, as it echoes backward and forward to what we have known. As we make room for these reverberations, we make room for preaching to align with its greatest hopes—namely, the hope that we move closer in proximity to that which is most holy and most true. This holy-truth is only clarified as it is named and recognized as such by the entire community, while *every* body contributes to arranging a choreography that responds to inspiration.

chapter 3
Mining Life for Preaching

If proclamation is the moment when something "rings true" and is recognized as an expression of the word of God in the community's midst, the content of the message must contain touch points with which listeners can make connections. Something is only considered true as it is recognized as such by listeners. A *yes!* and *amen!* affirms a moment in which we have named an utterance as valid or possessing authority. We recognize a message as valid because it possesses aspects of that which is familiar or discernable. This recognition is often facilitated through the places where we can draw lines to what a person intuits or believes as true.

We intuit what is valid based on what we have come to know through life. For instance, the experience of encountering and living out of grief and loss shapes what we know and believe as characteristically true about grief and loss, even as individuals and communities hold distinct and sometimes differing views of these two things. Life, our experiences, and our acquired knowledge are the barometers we use to measure the legitimacy of a message. Our barometers are made up of personal and collective experiences that facilitate our connection or lack of connection to any given sermon.

Listeners expect to hear something that relates to their ways of knowing, living, and moving about in the world. Preachers meet this expectation through narrating content that is familiar from everyday life. The use of personal and communal lived experiences creates and sustains points of connection between the faith claims and sacred texts present in a sermon. These points of connection manifest by way of places of illumination, stories, exemplification, and language that are familiar to those gathered.[1] There are various ways in which we may engage and articulate the closeness or distance between our message and the surrounding world. For instance, a preacher engaging a passage of scripture about lament and seeking to communicate something about lament to listeners may call forth experiences of grief, loss, and sorrow with which she suspects listeners are familiar.

When considering the distinctive of the experiences of black women in relation to preaching—in particular, their ways of knowing, living, and moving about in the world—the questions become "Whose experiences matter?" and "How are these experiences engaged for the purposes of preaching?" Engaging the experiences of black women as primary resources for preaching recovers narratives that are often ignored or minimally engaged in the process of shaping a community's collective beliefs and truths.

Black women's experiences are often not authorized or given authority as a community tells its history and story and tries to make sense of that history and story. For instance, one of the pervasive cultural narratives around the civil rights movement of the 1960s excludes the role and work of women in leadership while espousing the leadership of black men. Similarly, the cultural myth of the suffragist and women's movement did not bring to the forefront stories, needs, and experiences of black women. And at present day, the stories and leadership of black women who began the Black Lives Matter and Me Too movements were quickly erased and usurped by the voices and faces of others. The recovery of black women's experiences for the purposes of preaching begins moving the community outward and into a process of recovering narratives that are rendered invisible by the community.

As the experiences of black women are recovered, in its best practices this recovery makes room for the disregarded narratives of others. The lives of black women are a starting point for faithfully attending to the robustness of life and faith in a community. A preacher's ability to effectively engage life through preaching, as she calls forth unauthorized experiences or those that have been de-authorized by community, often requires a subtle and seamless weaving of new narratives and familiar narratives. Essentially, a preacher harnesses familiar experience as a resource for helping listeners imagine her message into their daily lives, even as this process of imagining involves listeners making points of connection with experiences that might not immediately be their own. During the sermon development process the preacher might think less about generic illustrations and instead consider the *right-fitness* of material for simultaneously authorizing silenced and ignored experiences while creating points of connection with the message.

Connections and Bridges to Life

The engagement of lived experience is the subtle yet poignant bridge between what is familiar and what is unfamiliar in preaching. A preacher must carve out a place for the reception of her message when helping a community imagine new possibilities. She does this by determining ways to use that which the community already knows to forge something new. Recognizing marginalized voices and experiences within the community, the preacher capitalizes on specific experiences that are already infused with a collective authority. We use existing communal language and memory alongside our own experience and wisdom as the first gateway into the process of imagining connections to our message. Multiple subjectivities meet here: those of the community, the preacher, and the tradition. And for black women, at this meeting place the histories of women's preaching traditions as subversive practices are retextured by the realities of living while black; and black preaching traditions are reshaped by the realities of black womanhood.

As human beings we have personal needs, experiences of faith, and encounters in this world that are shaped by the particularities of individual joys and sorrows. At its basic level, attending to that which is personal considers what it means to be human, the soul care required for any given individual, and what it requires for us to thrive as people. Historically, we have overly identified or compartmentalized the personal with pastoral care, evangelistic elements that emphasize personal belief, or self-help.

Engaging personal lived experiences entails recognizing that a community is made up of people attempting to make sense of their lives.

The personal stuff of what it means to be human is significant. However, these experiences are not separate from our connections to others, including our family and community, and broader interactions with society as a whole. In one sense our communal connections consist of shared and collective memories, experiences, and language that bond us to something larger than ourselves. This bond could be shaped alongside gendered, sexual, ethnic, and regional identities, creating a sense of similar stories and experiences with those sharing our space of belonging. Our collective concerns in life are sometimes narrated by corporate matters for well-being. These matters of well-being include how we thrive or obstacles to our thriving together. And when such concerns appear in preaching we often name them as justice oriented or prophetic.

Corporate concerns of existence land in concrete ways and influence personal suffering, soul care, and well-being.[2] For instance, economic disparities that create gaps in income among demographic groups are matters of corporate well-being. These same economic disparities land on the individual woman who does not have adequate access to healthcare, which creates a very distinct need of pastoral care. A message attending to both the personal and communal aspects of economic disparities offers both a corrective word to collective greed and a pastoral word for the acute emotional and phsyical dispair experienced by a person without healthcare.

In the best preaching practices, the personal and communal remain in conversation with each other, reflecting the lived realities of what it means to move about in the world, while facilitating points of connection between what listeners know and what is being said or introduced anew. These bridges to life are laid in very textured and concrete ways based on the community from which we preach.

(Re)Imaginings of the Familiar

Understandings of black preaching traditions rely heavily on communal language and memory or that which rings familiar. Something may ring familiar because it is a part of an oral history of a community. Something may ring familiar because it is a shared experience. Something may also ring familiar due to its hallmarks and the nature of its qualities, such as phrases and speech that have become parts of a group's lexicon and vernacular. In this regard communal language and memory can entail events, experiences, and rhetorical constructions. There are two underlying factors between these various components of the familiar. First, they are recognizable with little need of explanation. Second, they may also forge some type of a connection or alliance between individuals, even if only for a temporary time or moment of speech. Communal language and memory relies on both personal and collective ways of knowing.

When black women claim a vibrant subjectivity for the purposes of carving out places for their messages to connect with what is familiar to listeners, their retelling of the familiar expands the community's understanding of its language, memory, and experiences. The community recognizes that its borders and narratives are much more expansive than the ones it has previously recognized. Experiences that were cut out of the community now have the opportunity to be (re)imagined and grafted back into the community as they too become points of connection. For instance, foregrounding black womanhood becomes an interruption to a particular type of male preferential.

Configuring Celebration

Celebration is one gateway to reimagining the familiar through preaching. And this reimagining primarily takes place when celebration (tradition) intersects with the unapologetic experiences of black women (vibrant subjectivity). This meeting of tradition and vibrant subjectivity, at minimum, embraces a more elastic understanding of the familiar and whose experiences have value in a community.

Celebration occupies a great deal of space within conversations about black preaching traditions, to the extent that we often mistakenly understand it as the "gist" of black preaching. Celebration is not the totality of these preaching traditions, yet it remains a hallmark of some iterations of the tradition. Celebration has been described as encompassing the meeting of the mind, heart, and body in the message of a sermon.

Certainly there are other ways to think about how through preaching we seek to attend to the totality of our beings in their cognitive, emotional, physical, and spiritual dimensions. These other means may inspire hope without requiring a celebratory tone and structure. For instance, lament may be the more appropriate tenor for a message. As I explore celebration, the aim is not to reinforce assumptions that celebration must be a part of a sermon. Rather, we engage celebration here to see how even in highly structured expectations of preaching there is room to reshape those traditions through giving voice to the experiences of those least recognized. In contrast to the discussion of Rev. Barb's black jeremiad in chapter 2, here the emphasis is on the material of celebration as opposed to its performative aspects alone. The "stuff" that makes it up possesses great potential.

Celebration often relies on that which is familiar to a community. Multiple aspects of the familiar converge in celebration; it entails the presence of personal and communal ways of knowing, rhetorical phrases and structures that often go without saying, and it has the explicit intent of invigorating hope to continue to live out life in the world.[3] Celebration may occur near the end of a sermon, or its aims may influence the overall structure of any segment of the sermon as it shapes the arc of a segment through a "joyful and ecstatic reinforcement" of the message being conveyed.[4] The material of celebration often includes reference to scripture, including the crucifixion, familiar hymns, and the experiences of the preacher's and people's moments of conversion and experiences of God.[5] Stock formulas, which are recurring combinations of words and phrases within sermons between different preachers, may also appear in celebration. Some of these are traditionally understood as "set pieces"; namely, the sayings and phrases do not belong to one particular preacher but are open for public use and reuse without being considered plagiarism. An example of a stock formula in terms of the crucifixion would be "Didn't he, didn't he, didn't he die!" This formula invites listeners into the memory and affirmation that Jesus was crucified, usually just before the celebration and affirmation of the resurrection.[6] Celebration, its shared phrases, stock formulas, and set pieces include the presence of that which is formulaically familiar to a community and a part of its experiences while carrying forward the voices of those the community deem significant over time whether it is "the preacher of old" or grandmama's wisdom.

One of our preachers, Barbara, brings her sermon entitled "Are You Ready to Come to the Table" to an end in a more traditional understanding of celebration; she presents strong eschatological themes that include a named feminine presence. Her sermon is about the importance of appropriately preparing oneself for the communion table at present day. She creates the celebration with ideas of looking forward to a "great table," around which she and her listeners will gather in the future. In the excerpt that follows, Barbara solidifies her theme of preparation in a future hope and joy found in the presence of God and fellow saints:

> God just told me to tell you, If you are ready for this table, you'll be ready for that other great table! For John recorded, "Blessed are those who are invited to the wedding supper of the Lamb!"
>
> See, this communion feast is just like the rehearsal dinner before the wedding ceremony.
>
> I'm getting ready for that great table.
>
> I'm getting ready to feast with Abraham, Isaac, and Jacob!
>
> This is the table where I can *rub elbows with Mary and Martha!*
>
> The table where *all* of God's children have a place setting!
>
> And if that isn't all . . . I can look down to the head of the table and wave to Jesus!
>
> I want to be ready! I want to be ready to walk in that New Jerusalem!
>
> I want to be ready to see my Savior face to face!!
>
> I'VE GOT TO GET READY TO COME TO THE TABLE!!!!

Here, "getting ready" for the table and the point of celebration has dual implications: one for the present day and one for the future. The most celebratory aspect of the preparation of the preacher and listener is the assurance of being "ready" for the great feast, where they will sup with Jesus and familiar saints. The communion table Barbara is asking her listeners to prepare for is a "rehearsal dinner" for the "wedding supper of the Lamb," which will take place at the "great table!" At the great table, Barbara will be able "to look down to the head of the table and wave to Jesus!" She will not only feast with Abraham, Isaac, and Jacob, but also "rub elbows with Mary and Martha."

The ending of this sermon is intended to inspire and encourage listeners with hope as they continue to live out life at present day. The material she occupies this section with is of the most interest. Martha and Mary are the feminine presence, arguably unexpected at the "table where all of God's Children have a place setting!" The image of "rubbing elbows" almost conveys a very intimate and knowingly shared "we made it too" among Barbara, Martha, and Mary. Jesus is at the head of the table while all God's children are around him, solidifying her imagery of mutual belonging before God.

Barbara's celebration imagery is parallel to women's ways of knowing, historically, as it relates to place setting and arrangements at the table during a meal, and for black women the sharing of sisterhood, wisdom, and encouragement. Whether or not Barbara's use of Mary and Martha or place setting is intentional, the imagery conveys that "all God's children" include women and men and is not limited to the normative recitation of the patriarchal lineage of "Abraham, Isaac, and Jacob." Mary, Martha, and Barbara herself have a special setting at the meal.

If we were to reenvision Barbara's practice of celebration as an intentional (re)imagining of the familiar, she offers us insights about the opportunity to push this moment of improvisation further. As celebration is engaged by black women it may possess some communally expected content, including Jesus's life and crucifixion, excerpts from songs, hymns, and spirituals, shared communal sayings, and eschatological aspects. However, the use of the feminine and its appearance alongside and in combination with more expected content in both obvious and subtle ways is the most explicit form of ingenuity. The insertion of the feminine raises women's experiences as valid and a point of literal celebration within the community, even in what can seem to be a passing moment. Furthermore as the body carries forth the practice, women's literal bodies are recovered. One reason the preacher's insertion of feminine identity is successful here is because the feminine is inserted and employed within the confines of the familiar language and expected form of celebration. Within this practice, the tradition is not discarded but "signified on"[7] in different ways.

The subtlety of this practice belies its subversive potential. In one regard, as women continue and participate in the tradition of celebration, they interrupt the traditional imagery of the preacher by their embodiment as black and woman. The inclusion of the feminine in the language of celebration interrupts the traditional discourse of the practice itself and potentially interrupts the masculine ideals established by the tradition and safeguarded by community. The use of celebration by black women gains preachers a hearing with their listeners by using accepted and recognizable language forms, as it simultaneously raises women's experiences as valid within traditions that are male-preferential. In turn, the tradition of celebration becomes the means by which the feminine interrupts a tradition and style based on masculine ideals.

Expanding the Collective Experience

For iterations of black preaching traditions that do not ascribe to fully developed aspects of celebration, there are other ways by which a preacher might (re)imagine the familiar. I attended to the reality that life is shared earlier. In some sense the narrative and histories of "living while black" are a part of the shared life of members of black communities; and in preaching traditions, these narratives possess qualities of being an unwritten sacred story. In the following chapter, I will discuss the way in which this lived sacred story is interwoven with the written sacred story of scripture. Women preaching in these traditions have the ability to make use of living while black as a sacred story as they attend to the collective experience, not

chapter 3

as an experience of undistinguished individuals, but as an experience that holds the *experiences* of women, gender-nonconforming persons, children, and men—all of whom were affected in different ways by a historical narrative with contemporary implications.

Of our preachers, Sharon demonstrates this expansion of the collective in practice. In her sermon "The Tenacity of Humanity," which is based on the story of the Canaanite woman and her exchanges with Jesus in Matthew 15:21-28, Sharon parallels the "Canaanite problem," which Jesus finds himself "struggling with," to the "Black problem." Sharon recounts that the Canaanites had their homeland invaded and many of their people murdered and were forced into hard labor. She retraces "the tenacity of this race of people that survived after 1500 years of forced harsh slavery" and "flourished." She then simultaneously traces the history of African enslavement, their subsequent lives in the United States, and her uncertainty about whether or not "our race is heading for success or failure." The preacher addresses the social, political, and economic ills inflicted on black people in North America while "in the clutches of a destructive force." She does this by tracing events by the decade that have left indelible marks on black people in the United States.

During her sermon, Sharon speaks of fragmented families caused by a targeted draft for the Vietnam War in the 1960s and manipulative welfare distributions made by the government that gave increased incentives for men not living in the home during the 1970s. The preacher also laments the "unleashing" of crack, targeting women in the "projects leaving children without the watchful presence of mothers" during the 1980s. She acknowledges the suffering of black "young males" due to the rise of black-on-black crime during the 1990s and the media's simultaneous portrayal of their "overindulgence of drugs and alcohol" while promoting the false belief that it is more advantageous for black males to be in jail for increased life expectancy. She ultimately charges the community to not "give up" in being tenacious and to cry out based on their "faith," "freedom," and "victory in Christ, just as the Canaanite woman."

Sharon relies on and recounts the collective memory and experience of the "Black problem" to her listeners without losing the particular ways in which racism has affected different groups of black people, including children, women, and men. Sharon also attends to those who could be easily lost in the story: the women and the children. For Sharon, the black problem is not just the black male problem; it is the problems of black children, black women, and black men; and she recounts their experiences while specifying each one.

If we were to reenvision Sharon's use of the community's sacred stories as an intentional (re)imagining of the familiar, the ingenuity in preaching this way entails the choices made in terms of whose experiences are foregrounded in creating touch points or points of illumination in the sermon. The known story of living while black is very much present, as it is also retold for the sake of including the experiences of black women and children. In this use of the familiar the re-grafting of other missing experiences is made possible, such as those of children who are often made the most invisible in the community, as the preacher unequivocally claims women's experiences in these trajectories. The already authorized sacred story is the vehicle that recapitulates ways of knowing that the community might not readily acknowledge. The story more fully becomes *our story* in this process. Ingenuity is not about black women transgressing preaching practices with the implications being reserved for their greater welfare alone, though sometimes this is sufficient; but more accurately there are implications for the welfare of the community writ large.

Calling Forth Prophets, Poets, and Wisdom Bearers

Finding sources of truth telling, proclamation, and wisdom outside of preaching and the Christian narrative itself is not uncommon in the history of black life. We only need to consider the blues, jazz, hip hop, literary, and cultural arts and other expressive mediums by which black lived experience and the process of codifying it have taken shape over time.[8] Cultural prophets, poets, and wisdom bearers are interwoven in the history of black life and black preaching traditions. The voices of these individuals are recognized as carrying weight, authority, or the uncanny ability to crystalize truths that are part and parcel to black life. Their voices are trusted with the work of narrating the familiar. Because of their recognition by the community, they are the individuals who are "voiced" as authority figures. Their recognition is not about the individual alone but also about an understanding and acceptance of the wisdom and truth they embody.

For instance, *grandmama* might be an iconic enough relationship with its own legacy that the invocation of the name gives whoever is filling that role in the moment the authority to speak and have influence on thought and opinions. Therefore, even if there is a disintegrated understanding of a rigid preaching tradition and a collective narrative present in a community, there remains the presence of cultural prophets, poets, and wisdom bearers; and these figures may be used for the work of (re)imagining the familiar, especially when their voices are used to give others voice.

In the sermons of Patricia, Sharon, and Valerie, Martin Luther King Jr., is a recurring figure; so too are fragments from his speeches and *Letter from a Birmingham Jail*:

> So often we need to be led to the mountain—a place where God can have your attention. . . . Even when MLK was in Memphis—He said that he didn't know what was going to happen to him but he knew tough times were ahead. But it didn't matter, because he have been to the mountaintop. —Patricia

> I share in this title "Why We Can't Wait" from Martin Luther King Jr. while in a Birmingham prison wrote a letter. . . . MLK responded that they could no longer wait. . . . God told the disciples to wait but after that it was time for them to fulfill the commission to go into the world and be agents of change. —Sharon

> In the New Testament, Jesus explicitly connected discipleship with social concern and cited compassion of the needy as one measure by which he would recognize his followers. It was the prophet Dr. Martin Luther King Jr., who said, "Injustice anywhere is injustice everywhere." . . . Yet, we sit here in all our piety and yet people in Nashville went to bed hungry last night, others slept with only the stars in the sky as their covering. —Valerie

Patricia, Sharon, and Valerie use Martin Luther King, Jr., to narrate the significance of working for social change as a part of discipleship. They emphasize that social change and action cannot wait because people are in need in the surrounding communities; the challenges are difficult, but they are a part of their Christian responsibility.

While MLK Jr. may seem like an obvious choice, cultural prophets, poets, and wisdom bearers can take other forms, such as Marvin Gaye. It would not be uncommon for preachers to engage faith, crime, natural disaster, and social and political woes through the songs of Gaye and others:

> The Christian journey is riddled with busted situations that *make us want to holler and throw up both of our hands!*
>
> Then again on Tuesday evening, CNN reported an earthquake in Sumatra, India, that registered 7.9! *Like Marvin I asked, "what's going on?"*
> —Barbara

For Barbara, in her sermons, Gaye is the "go to" artist and prophet; his songs help her articulate a message in relevant and recognizable terms.

However, prophets, poets, and wisdom bearers do not end at iconic figures; instead, voices of ordinary people can have just as great of an influence as they occupy roles of communal sages. For instance, "Like the old folk used to say, if it ain't one thing it's another." Another variation of *the old folk* is *the saints*, as in Patricia's use here:

> You may think that God has forgotten about you . . . But I am here to tell you that God did not forget you. . . . Wait on the Lord.
>
> *The saints used to tarry.* Tarry means to wait. The saints used to wait on the Holy Ghost to come in or wait for something from the Lord. . . . They began to call on the name of Jesus [express it]. . . . There is power in the Name of Jesus. . . . Great things began to happen, but they had to wait on the Lord. —Patricia

The use of *the saints* and *the old folk* pulls on the imputed knowledge of the elders about the trials and difficulties of life and life in faith. As Patricia communicates a validation of the experiences of life being difficult due

chapter 3

to repeated trials, she uses the elders as credible witnesses to her words as she exhorts. And it is not uncommon for these saints to be elder women of wisdom such as *mama* and *grandmama*. Vicki demonstrates the use of mama in her sermon entitled "Oil for Pouring":

> *My mother used to say*, Where you show out is where you get wo' out" and right here all the negative, backbiters get helped by Jesus. He says, "Leave her alone. She has done what she could." —Vicki

Vicki's mother's voice is the voice that gives warning that we are corrected, disciplined, and chastised in the same places and instances in which we do inappropriate things: "Where you show out is where you get wo' out." The preacher then uses her mother's voice to amplify and support her claim that Jesus is correcting ("helping") the "negative backbiters" who have acted inappropriately. In this instance, mother's voice and wisdom are the support for the preacher's claim. *Grandmama* and *mama* are established and respected wisdom bearers whose voices matter not only to the women but also in their community. They are a part of the great cloud of witnesses that includes the elder saints within the preachers' communities.

Grandma and mama are regarded as cultural prophets and poets just as much as Marvin Gaye and Martin Luther King Jr. However, grandmothers and mothers are a part of a larger strand of the feminine as voiced wisdom and expert testimony, which includes women in mainstream media, academia, and the creative arts used in order to validate and support the veracity of a message. Vicki is the most astute in her variety and use of the "expert" black women. She uses Emilie Townes, Valerie Bridgeman, and Renita Weems, all credentialed womanist educators of religion and theology, to address the plight and struggle of young black girls and children who have suffered violence and sexual abuse:

> Tamar lived in patriarchal times and within a situation of life far different from our lives today. Our response to sexual violence within our family does not have to be the same as hers. Dr. Valerie Bridgeman Davis suggests that while "it is unfortunate that Tamar's community forced her to carry the guilt and shame and forced her to live her life as

a desolate woman living in her bother Absalom's house," that does not have to be our present reality. —Vicki

Here, Vicki uses Bridgeman, a Hebrew Bible scholar, not only as a voice, but as a voice that challenges the community to offer a different response in real life than the one narrated in scripture. The preacher uses the expert as a voice that gives her the authority to essentially preach against the text. In another instance, Vicki literally uses the prayer and blessing of Baby Suggs, holy, the fringe itinerant preacher in Toni Morrison's *Beloved*,[9] to preach for her and "close" the sermon:

> Finally, we must embrace the holiness and sacredness of loving ourselves by connecting to spiritual truths like those found in Baby Sugg's prayer and blessing for the people in Toni Morrison's Beloved. She told them that the only grace they could have was the grace they could imagine. That if they could not see it, they would not have it. —Vicki

Through the voice of Baby Suggs, holy, Toni Morrison challenges gathered listeners to imagine and create grace in the flesh during their lives in this world. In her sermon, Vicki has challenged listeners to take seriously the injustices committed against the flesh of innocent bodies and to correct those injustices. Thus, Morrison and Baby Suggs, holy, become the individuals through whom Vicki gives rise to her voice, and they ultimately conclude the sermon.

When the preachers use cultural prophets and poets such as Grandmama, Mama, King, Gaye, and Baby Suggs, holy, they close the gap between the sacred and secular. For these preachers, there is something to be claimed as sacred within the ordinary speech, songs, and writings that are a part of their communities. When the preachers make explicit choices to include the external voices of black women as wisdom bearers, they not only invite and participate in a larger tradition of black women handing on spiritual values and moral wisdom across generations,[10] but also they bring the voices of black women into the midst for the community's engagement.

As we turn to (re)imagining the familiar, the spoken and written words of others are often the means through which preachers establish credibility in their messages and give rise to their own voices, utilizing women and men who are acknowledged and respected within their communities in order to speak to their communities of faith. Yes, the use of others to vouch for one's authority is not a novel phenomenon in preaching; however, who preachers choose to use is of real importance.

Ingenuity and Everyday Life

As preachers attend to the expectation and place of familiar experience in sermons, their own and their listeners' life world are integral parts of sermon content. Preachers rely heavily on the community's language and memory, whether by recalling the collective experiences and language of the community or by creating common points of experience around which the community can engage. As another means of using that which is familiar, preachers might conjure the recognized voices of others within their sermons as a means of giving voice to their own faith claims. What becomes worthy of noting is when black women engage the traditions and language of the community alongside the feminine. For the preachers featured here, the persona of being black and a woman is best conveyed in the simultaneous attention to cultural products attached to their ethnic identity and communities as well as their sometimes very apparent engagement with feminine experiences. There are a myriad of other forms in which this parallel of the communal and feminine highlighted might occur.

Historically, interruption is an aspect of women's preaching traditions. Eunjoo Mary Kim traces the theology and practice of women preachers from the early church through the twentieth century and discusses how the particulars of feminine experiences influence the content and theology of preaching.[11] For instance, as a result of analyzing the sermons of women preachers in the medieval and post-medieval church, Kim found key rhetorical strategies used by women who "gave their unique voice to the masculine-oriented church and their respective societies."[12] Kim notes patterns through which these women[13] use "allegories, tricks, imaginative language and feminine imagery of God" for the purpose of communicating the gospel.[14] These rhetorical strategies of women preachers are significant because they interject feminine experience and imagery into otherwise masculine and patriarchal contexts and conceptualizations of God. Kim argues that women's preaching as subversive rhetoric takes seriously inclusive language and female imagery of God as it seeks egalitarianism—all while requiring subtlety, training, and exploratory approaches.[15]

The feminine experience itself is a means of interruption in preaching; and at times this interruption is more intentionally engaged through purposefully subversive acts that recognize and call forth the feminine experience. Black women's preaching that concretely claims its location engages personal and communal memories and experiences at the intersections of being both black and woman. And often, neither identification as black or woman escapes the preacher's grasp, interrupting any understanding of a binary between the identities of black and womanhood. In preaching that claims such a vibrant subjectivity, *Sophia*, the personification of wisdom, is the black woman whose voice is perpetually repeated through the voices of other black women. As black women are the voices in the preaching moment that occupy the pulpit, they simultaneously invite and make room for the feminine voice that comes from within the larger community's tradition of lived wisdom. As the preachers themselves embody a privileged space, they invite other women into that space to bear witness and to make proclamation with them—broadening the meadow.

(Re)Imagining Sermon Development

As preachers ascertain and demonstrate a deep knowledge of their communities while engaging the tradition of the gathered community, this knowledge and tradition becomes the point from which they pivot to connect with the daily life world of listeners. This use of the familiar is personal and communal at its core, providing multiple opportunities for listeners to make points of connection with scripture, the message, and faith claims.

In order to use familiar experience in this manner, the preacher must first of all directly engage their knowledge of the gathered community and human experience. This engagement includes exploring communal language and memory through the shared narratives, joys, and struggles of the community, or *finding communal sacred stories*. Second, the preacher must learn to call forth the values, assumptions, and authority located within the voiced of the community, which I refer to as *recovering the voiced*. As we will see, stories and voices are a part of every community's tradition, and they are often the vehicles of that tradition. Third, for the preacher seeking to continue tradition in transformed ways, they must learn to place their own experiences and the experiences of others alongside dominant communal language and memory.

This placing alongside of has the potential to interrupt and expand the shape and content of that which is recognizable and familiar within the community, otherwise known as *using the familiar to transform the familiar*. Lastly, preachers must learn to gather up the daily struggles and joys of human experience, both personal and corporate, in a way that creates shared ways of knowing in the midst of a gathered community, or *creating mutual experiences*. Creating mutual experiences and conveying truth are nearly inseparable. For this reason, I will not treat this method of using familiar experience in the following section. Instead, I will engage the process of creating mutual experience in chapter 5 when I discuss the process by which we create meaning through preaching. *Finding communal sacred stories, recovering the voiced, using the familiar to transform the familiar,* and *creating mutual experiences* all create opportunities for a community to experience the authority and significance of the gospel in its immediate context and language.

Finding the Community's Sacred Stories

Sacred stories are narratives deemed valuable within in a specific community, based on their repetition and force of meaning within that community (i.e., these preaching women's use of the various iterations of the narrative of "living while black"). As preachers utilize sacred stories, they call forth the language and memory that belongs to the community in which they preach. The use of sacred stories creates a mutual point of identification during the sermon between both the preacher and listeners and amongst the listeners themselves.[16] In addition to identification, the use of sacred stories deploys the language and memory most familiar to the community for the purposes of determining what is meaningful in that context. We communicate a meaningful message and facilitate connections with our message through speaking "the language of the folk" and reduce the possible obstacles in a listener's ability to apprehend the significance and authority of a message.

In preaching, we seek to minimize the potential obstacles that inhibit the message's communication, which includes obstacles created through language and symbols that are distant from the language and symbols of a community. Lenora Tubbs Tisdale writes about preaching as an act of engaging local theology and folklore, in that the preacher must take the time to know and understand the community in which she preaches.[17] Preaching itself is an act of folklore in so far as its language, symbols, illustrations, and form remain close to the "ground of the people."[18] Specifically, Tisdale compares preaching to circle folk dancing.[19] The preacher's use of the folk's language encourages listeners to meet the preacher and participate with them in the event of the sermon: the circle folk dance. To an extent, preaching is cross-cultural communication; varying cultures are present amongst listeners as well as between listeners and the preacher.[20]

Through their use of the everyday life world of the congregation, the preacher minimizes potential obstacles inherently present within preaching as a cross-cultural act, while forging something that is immediate and specific. As the preacher becomes more proficient in understanding the culture of the congregation, they gain access to the local knowledge of the community. Tisdale suggests that preachers can access this knowledge through congregational stories and interviews, archival collections, demographics, architecture and visual arts, rituals, events and activities, and people counted as influential and having wisdom.[21] As the preacher then becomes proficient in their utilization of that knowledge for preaching, preaching becomes something of a "local theology" for a "very particular" group of people in a "very particular" time and space.[22] This form of preaching creates a common language between preacher and listeners as well as amongst listeners themselves: it is listener oriented and proclaims something "to," "out of the mist," and "on behalf" of those present.[23]

Excellent preachers are also ethnographers; they know and understand the culture of their preaching environment and are then able to utilize that understanding in sermon development and design.[24] Insider knowledge becomes central in this type of preaching, as the preacher interprets the "signs and symbols" of a community[25] based on time spent engaging the community. To an extent, insider knowledge supports both the authority of the preacher as an insider demonstrating belonging and understanding, and the message as it is conveyed in the language and symbols of the community. Those who preach as perceived outsiders are participating in a particularly textured form of cross-cultural communication. The ability to make use of the language and symbols of the community at hand is their first bridge across the divide.

IN PRACTICE
Finding the Community's Sacred Stories

Here are practical helps for exploring events, stories, and memories that are significant in the life of a community.

1. Write down significant events and stories in the life of the community. This attention to community accounts for community in its most immediate and broadest capacities. In thinking about events and stories, consider those that have occurred in the past year, five years, ten years, and so on.

2. Out of those events, consider events that have special meaning, demonstrated through the community's retelling of these stories over and over again. Give attention to events acknowledged as significant by many members of the community and also by a smaller fraction of the community.

3. After pinpointing these stories, consider from whose point of view the stories are told. This begins the process of thinking about various ways to deploy the narratives in preaching or, better yet, expand those narratives through preaching.

Recovering the Voiced

As an extension of knowing the culture of the community within which they preach, preachers rely on their knowledge of those who are voiced within the community. The voiced of the community includes those acknowledged as influential, credible, and authoritative, such as grandmama, saints of old, wisdom bearers, cultural prophets, and poets. Preachers often rely on the words, phrases, terminology, and works of the voiced to provide the backing and warrant for the claims they are making. By making use of the idioms of these voices, a preacher opens up the opportunity for their voice to be heard and received as credible within the community. This acknowledgment and use of the voiced is of real importance for individuals who may struggle to find a voice or possess a contested voice within their communities.

Significant people and symbols constitute a crucial vehicle for communicating values within a community. As Tisdale advocates for cultural ethnography and exegesis as a primary aspect of preaching, she notes that certain people, both assuming and unassuming presences, can "symbolically personify ideals of the community."[26] Such people communicate the community's values, but they also show where the in-group and out-group boundaries exist and can simultaneously function as cohesion, healing, and wholeness within a community.[27] In particular, Tisdale notes two groups of individuals being of importance: sages and those "on the margins." On the one hand, the sages possess an "elusive" wisdom, often enacting or displaying the values of a congregation, sometimes functioning in influential leadership roles, and at other times providing "healing and wholeness" within the community. On the other hand, those on the margins may be those who "don't fit in" or who are considered to be "extreme or eccentric" individuals who color outside the normative boundary lines of a community.[28] Community values are reinforced by people as well as transmitted through people.

The use of voice and speech is one way through which people transmit community values. The ability to give voice and to use one's voice is an authoritative expression.[29] Mary Lin Hudson and Mary Donovan Turner explain: "Exercising one's right to speak says something about the power and value of authorizing one's own perspective."[30] There is value claimed in one's experience, reason, and reflection when an individual speaks and makes public that experience, reason, and reflection.[31] Plainly stated, "Voice has value." Most congregations allow certain voices to speak and have formational privilege within the community, be it through the community's response to that voice or through the repetition of that voice. Embracing these voices communicates both that the community grants authority to those particular voices and that certain voices are in some way recognized as authoritative reflections of the community's values. Therefore, a tactical use of the power and authority of voice by those whose voices are marginalized (i.e., women in contested spaces or LGBTQIA+ individuals in heterosexist spaces) is for the preacher to use already established credible and authoritative voices in the community, in order to bolster their authority as they seek to gain a listening from those who may not be receptive to their voice and perspective.

IN PRACTICE
Recovering the Voiced

Here are some practical helps for recovering and making use of voices present within the community.

1. Jot down those who are considered wisdom bearers for the community (again, considering *community* in its most immediate and broadest capacity). When thinking of wisdom bearers and those who have voice, consider those who are often quoted; consider important familiar figures; consider those viewed and acknowledged as "experts" in various areas or with certain life knowledge.

2. List actual phrases that are often said or known within the community. Take another minute to quickly write down *who* comes to mind when you hear each phrase (i.e., who actually says this?).

3. Say these phrases and explore the idiom. Record them if you can and listen to them in your own voice.

4. Write down *what* first comes to mind thematically when you hear each phrase (*hope, faith, life, uncertainty, jealousy, greed, happiness*, etc.).

Using the Familiar to Transform the Familiar

At times, preachers may need to use that which is familiar and recognizable to listeners as the means to interrupt aspects of the traditions they engage. As preachers both are aware of and utilize the community's sacred stories and the credible voices of the community, they also make use of their own experiences and the experiences of those on the fringes of the community, making the familiar over again as new (i.e., the use of the feminine in celebration and the use of women, children, and men in the experience of "living while black"). By using experience in this way, a preacher introduces new or counter-traditional content along with that which is familiar to the community. In this way, we explore the ways in which the already familiar may be used to expand and interrupt tradition. The community's tradition and the preacher's way of knowing then become the site of creative engagement, riffing off of the tradition to create something similar to, yet different from, the recognized tradition. These moments demonstrate the possibility of using established communal language and memory to transform communal beliefs and tradition.

As I discussed earlier, signs, symbols, and people are conduits of a tradition and that which is familiar and most valued within the community. One of the larger aims in preaching, however, is to move beyond the business of reinforcing already-existing norms. The larger aim in preaching is to use the common and conventional to transform or to forge something new within the life of the community. The preacher has to distance herself a bit from her "insider" position with the community and gain access to the critical edge that comes with her "outsider" and more distanced relationship with the community.[32] The gospel proclaimed pushes the community beyond itself and that which is familiar to the community into a greater vision. The familiar becomes the imaginative vehicles through which the gospel then transforms the community.

For instance, the parables of Jesus engaged the familiar concepts, images, world, and speech of the community, yet they pushed the community's imagination and view beyond its current place in time. In a similar manner, preaching can also expand the community's values, limits, and imagination. This expansion is accomplished through inverting the assumed

chapter 3

ordering of the community's world: challenging false and troublesome values within the community while opening up unimagined possibilities within the same community. The key to this transformational aspect of preaching is the use of common language, experience, and the world of the community as the vehicle of transformation.

It is important to bear in mind that the preacher's ability to narrate an understanding of the tradition to listeners is of real importance if they hope to transform a tradition. The preacher is able to establish their credibility as a competent preacher who knows the tradition and narrative of the community as they engage the narratives, traditions, and key voices of the community. The insider credibility they establish by acknowledging the legitimacy of narrative and tradition simultaneously creates room for their own experiences and knowing to interrupt and possibly transform the tradition. The ability to potentially subvert and transform the tradition "as is" is based largely on the preacher's ability to gain a listening heart by first finding common ground or points of solidarity with listeners.

IN PRACTICE
Using the Familiar to Transform the Familiar

Here are some practical steps in moving towards using the familiar for the sake of expanding or transforming traditions:

1. Brainstorm the ways in which the easily recognizable or familiar is usually expressed in sermons to the community. (For example, is the familiar usually conveyed via story, song, quotes, passing phrases, or celebration?)

2. Revisit the "IN PRACTICE" section on "Recovering the Voiced" of the community. In looking over the voiced within the community, consider alternative figures who may not be well known but who have the characteristics of these wisdom bearers. (For instance if Martin Luther King Jr. is a recognized wisdom bearer marked by leadership characteristics and community mobilization, Septima Poinsette Clark may be an alternative wisdom bearer.)

3. In the same "IN PRACTICE" section, review the phrases and quotes identified as reoccurring within the community; note any problems and disagreements you experience with those phrases. If there are points of disagreement with the phrases, consider counterimages or counter phrases to place alongside those phrases.

4. In a similar manner, revisit the "IN PRACTICE" section in which you located the community's sacred narratives. Consider who is usually left unattended in the story.

5. Now, think about *transformation*. Where might counter or alternative stories, images, voices, and phrases be combined with, intersect, or make new these normal means of expressing the familiar?

••

This process of exploring familiar experience helps us gain access to both wisdom about the community in which we preach and wisdom about human experience. Actively naming and calling forth familiar experiences helps retain the information for quick accessibility when making connections among familiar experience, scripture, constructing meaning, and sacred storytelling.

Using the Familiar as a Resource

Preaching is in constant conversation with the ways in which individuals and communities attempt to make sense of their lives in this world. This conversation relies on what is familiar to listeners as they move about in life. Ultimately, our way of knowing is an existence and reality connected to others. We only know what we have known previously or have come to know presently. Therefore, even the ability to shape new belief and new possibilities for the ways in which we exist in the world echoes back, intersects, and makes connections to that which is currently or formerly known. With this in mind, preachers use that which is familiar as a resource in preaching.

chapter 3

Preaching that seeks to make way for new possibilities, including new avenues in preaching practice and belief, uses that which is familiar as a bridge to the unfamiliar. In short, preaching relies on connections between similarities and dissimilarities for forging imaginative futures not yet experienced. A message and preaching practice that makes way for the acceptance of new voices galvanizes its support by utilizing facets of that which already exists—*the familiar*.

When black women preach they often engage the familiar—even the familiar experiences of their listeners—to help (re)imagine that which is familiar into something more or different. Knowing the significance of personal and communal language and memory as used in everyday life is essential for this work of (re)imagining, as one claims a vibrant subjectivity. As personal identity is always in conversation with communal identity, the work of the preacher is to claim her personal identity even as she does the work of naming for the purpose of attending to the personal and collective concerns of the community. In this, she makes room for the ongoing claiming and expanding of identities in her community. However, as the preacher begins with her experience as a starting point it is not the final destination. Instead, the preacher's lived experience becomes a bridge for imagining ways to connect with others and helping others imagine themselves into the message. This imagining is particularly significant for those who have been displaced or forced to the outer edges of a community.

chapter 4
Recovering Sacred Texts for Preaching

Preaching within communities of faith may be understood as one aspect that makes way for the opportunity to experience sacred utterances. These sacred utterances are typically described as word of God and are an experience of proclamation. In this regard, preaching assumes the ability of a community to encounter significant and meaningful revelation in its midst. Yet preaching beckons such revelation without guarantee of it occurring. The revelation is dependent upon a synergistic meeting of the spirit, the community, and the preacher. In a similar manner, scripture is a text that any given community deems sacred precisely because of its historical role in facilitating an encounter with meaningful revelation.

Communities of faith have come to know scripture as *word of God* because the text has been a touch point for accessing divine revelation—or a meaningful disclosure of truth. As preaching itself makes way for sacred utterances, the way in which a preacher makes use of scripture through preaching is often associated with not only revelation but also the means by which a community legitimizes the preaching of an individual. When we preach we are in a constant negotiation with the value a community places on scripture.

How we attend to scripture is all the more significant when: (1) a community deems scripture as holy writ and largely unquestionable; (2) scripture has been used to silence or exclude the full inclusion of some individuals within a community; and (3) scripture exists as a legitimate conduit of divine revelation that has contemporary significance. Often, there are portions of scripture that may not be *word of God* on many days for those who are marginalized within a community, as it does not support their inclusion, thriving, or flourishing within the life of the community. Yet, those same texts are valued as sacred within a community. Passages of scripture that seem to promote violence, the second-class citizenship of women and others, purposeful suffering, and the innate insufficiency or evil of an individual all loom threats on our ongoing life together. This is particularly true when such texts intersect with symmetrical social narratives about black women. When black women preach they are mediating two encounters with scripture—namely, their encounter and the wider community's encounter.

Those who preach as perceived outsiders have a particularly significant vantage point for interpreting scripture for preaching. The preacher negotiates a reinterpretation of tradition, present-day beliefs, and the inherent value a community of faith gives its sacred texts. This negotiation in interpreting scripture is often entangled with enigmas and threats to the ongoing survival of the preacher and others when preachers proclaim from the fringes, where many black women proclaim. Preaching necessitates being astute in knowing when and how to use caution and to take liberties in interpretive decisions, while both life and scripture are held as sacred texts.

The preacher's identity is not secondary in the art of interpreting scripture for preaching, but primary. The best practices of preaching account for and acknowledge where and how the preacher enters the process. In order to account for her point of entry, the preacher claims a vibrant subjectivity at the forefront of approaching a text. And just as in the use of familiar experience, one does not claim a vibrant subjectivity for the sake of ending at her own story and experience but for the sake of accounting for her own biases and inclinations, with hopes of eventually imagining how others may enter the story alongside her.

Both scripture and life are sacred texts that remain connected in the preaching of black women. In their use of these sacred texts, black-preaching-women rely on the communal assumption that the purposes of preaching and the use of scripture are for the sake of experiencing a word from the Lord that means something for me today. And ultimately, this assumption includes the lives of black women, which means neither the word from the Lord nor interpretation of scripture through preaching can be undermining of the ongoing lives and flourishing of black women. Preaching and scripture are for the sake of sustaining life itself.

Interplay and Play

Interpreting scripture requires the preacher to discover points of slippage, movement, or connection between the world of the text and her world; these points are sites of interplay. In preaching we attend to the chasm among when, for what purposes, and for whom the stories of a text were once rendered, and how a text might ring anew. We approach scripture in search of relationships between two worlds—the ancient and contemporary worlds. The assumption is that scripture has something to say for here and now as it carries forward remnants of its past hopes. Uncovering these moments of connection between the present and past requires a type of literal play in our interactions with a text. The word *play* here does not denote a lack of earnestness and intention, while it does denote a disposition of openness and attentiveness to the joy of discovering unknown possibilities in the exchange. Scripture brings its histories into the presence of the one it engages; and the one who engages scripture brings her life and history into the presence of scripture. In these meeting spaces interplay and play occur.[1]

Black preaching traditions have always allowed room for the presence of active play and interplay. Henry Mitchell described interpretive processes in black preaching traditions as "gospel, not science."[2] The premise of gospel, not science is an attempt to describe how black preaching at its best avoids both interpretations of texts that are too literalist, leading to intellectual dead ends, and interpretations that are complete flights of fancy without any tethering to the historical and intellectual. In these interpretive frameworks the historical, factual, and text itself are placed into a creative service to the life of faith. Both life and scripture are sacred texts that help make the good news evident. When good news for the sake of life is at stake, the play and interplay among text, preacher, and listeners make way for various interpretive outcomes. In turn, black women can make use of these interpretive possibilities for what they deem as the good news at stake, which may even lead to the necessity of (re)imagining the sources and possibilities of that good news.

Most important, our encounter with scripture helps concretize in some way the saving effect of the gospel on life today.[3] This salvific activity is the process of interrupting and rescuing us from the loop of literal damnations that prevent our flourishing as created holy-infused beings. Scripture continues as a living document in our midst. Its organic possibilities are made manifest as it intermingles with the contemporary demands and constraints of what it means to exist and move about in the present world.

The existence of our individual and collective living are always in flux. And therefore, the interpretation of scripture is not a static or fixed revelation. The interpretation of scripture is a constantly dynamic process. Meanings of scripture are always tied to our abilities to understand and experience scripture here and now. There is not one meaning of scripture; we derive meanings in interaction with scripture. In our best practices of interpreting scripture for preaching, these meanings are refractions of one gospel that makes itself manifest in our midst, as it is discerned by the entire community. The key here is the constant interplay among understanding, meaning, and communal discernment.

(Re)Imaginings of Texts

Assumptions within preaching traditions about both the accessibility of scripture and the role of lived wisdom in interpreting scripture are significant points of entry for black women who preach. A community's encounter with scripture is often facilitated on the premise of relationship. The primary relationship is one with God, which influences the approach to scripture as one in search of an encounter with a divine being who is known and wants to be known.[4] The secondary relationship is between the text and lives of people of faith, which assumes a type of familiarity with scripture in terms of the ability for scripture to be known and its desire to be known. There is an ownership of encountering the Bible through preaching that affords scripture to be re-presented for the sake of vouching for and re-inscribing both its accessibility and disclosure of good news for today.

In some black preaching traditions, this relational phenomenon is described as *the Bible as my story*[5]—that is, the story of black people. The Bible as my story names the ability of the community to engage the Bible as an entity to which they have capacity to connect and understand through a give-take relational exchange. Interpretation of the Bible through preaching assumes a type of intimacy with the text.

The process by which black women engage scripture for preaching is (re)cast when we place intimate frameworks of interpreting scripture in conversation with black women's ways of moving about in the world. Namely, the preacher makes use of the authority a community gives both scripture and lived wisdom in interpreting texts. And the ways in which she engages scripture is the means by which communities that are often hostile, or agnostic, toward her presence are able to experience her interpretations of scripture as *sacred utterances*. In this approach, the preacher does not discard the text in preaching, even those texts that are difficult; instead she builds upon present assumptions about interpretive practices for her own purposes. This particular use of the text in turn attests to the legitimacy of her preaching, in contrast to the ways in which discarding the text might undermine her preaching in a community resistant to her presence. And in this particular turn, the Bible moves from *my story* to *our story* in the most fullest sense of *our*.

The preacher offers listeners the ability to encounter scripture as she rhetorically instantiates the close or more distant relationship between scripture and their lived experiences. At any point, life or scripture may trade off some of its authority for the other. The permission listeners grant preachers to creatively move between ancient and contemporary worlds and the practices of meticulously engaging texts to demonstrate theses porous boundaries, makes possible both facilitating points of connection with scripture and expanding foci of a community when engaging scripture. This expansion may include one of the most difficult tasks, which is the task of preaching against, instead of in support of, a text. Such decisions are necessary when a text is not beneficial to the ongoing life and thriving of the community. Preaching against a text must be enacted when a specific interpretation of a text *cannot be a word from the Lord* that means something for me today. However, before a preacher can move against the text, she has to determine how to build upon that which already resonates with listeners.

Fluidity between Worlds

The fulcrum for shifting and shaping ongoing practice and belief within a community lies at the point of identification or resonance with an idea. Yet the greatest hurdle to creating these moments of identification when engaging scripture is the preacher's ability to help listeners envision the relationship between scripture and life. This envisioning might be facilitated as the preacher makes choices in narrating that which is familiar to listeners into, out of, and by scripture throughout the sermon.

When familiar experience is narrated *out of scripture*, experience functions as the dominant theme. Daily life holds the most authority and greatly influences how scripture is used and engaged in the sermon. The major objective is to "show life" within scripture, and in these occurrences, scripture is the "see here, this is what we experience" mirror that reflects daily life. Narrating familiar experience out of scripture can be done as a form of validation or affirmation in order to normalize a life experience. It can be done in a way that explains or answers an existing question or concern in life, as well as refutes or corrects a daily life experience.

For instance, when preachers use scripture to validate, affirm, or support the experiences of daily life, daily life is the organizing principle of the sermon content at hand. As daily life organizes the sermon content, scripture functions as the mechanism of support in order to verify or give validity to the experience with which the preacher is engaging. Louise's sermon "Postponement and Reconciliation" provides one example of this approach undertaken in a sermon. In the sermon she portrays an African American woman not wanting to reveal her racial-ethnic identity at a trade show event for fear of such a revelation affecting the sales of her product, which is presumably based on past experience; the story line is one of the sermon's touch points to everyday life. Her primary scripture reference is John 11:1-45, which recounts Jesus's encounter with Mary and Martha in the resurrection of Lazarus from the dead. She explains that this is a story that reveals something about life:

> This is another of the familiar stories from scripture. It is a story that reveals to us that sometimes in life, things do not turn out the way we expected. . . . It is a story that touches our lives in so many points along the journey of life. . . . I believe that I see through the actions of Jesus postponement and reconciliation. —Louise

Louise makes it explicitly known that the text "reveals" something about life's experiences. She contends that scripture shows and affirms "that sometimes in life, things do not turn out the way we expected." Louise uses the story in scripture to confirm and normalize her listeners' experiences along the "journey of life," specifically the times when things do not turn out as expected. Jesus himself is the one who narrates these experiences in what she calls "postponement and reconciliation."

Later in the sermon, with the story of a friend's decision to "come out" about her racial-ethnic identity, Louise makes a turn to show how life experience is mirrored in scripture and how scripture is mirrored in life experience. In using her friend's experience, Louise makes the turn to say essentially, "See this is what is happening here in life and scripture; see the realities of delay; see the potential of confusing delay with permanent denial; and see delay not meaning denial." Without saying these words explicitly, the preacher explains, gives voice to, and validates a familiar experience by the way she constructs the relationship between scripture and daily life. Jesus's delayed arrival to the bedside of Lazarus, which resulted in his death but later his resurrection, is connected to our contemporary experiences of delayed resolution in life's circumstances. For Louise, scripture's value and her faith claims must be connected to the daily life struggles of living with faith. Most important, scripture is the means for validating listeners' everyday experiences, and those experiences hold valid authority in the interpretive process.

chapter 4

Narrating lived experiences *by* scripture is more direct than narrating experience *out of* scripture. When we narrate experience *by scripture*, we place authority most constantly *in* scripture, as opposed to the interchange between the authority of scripture and the authority of the daily life world that are often found in the patterns of narrating experience out of scripture. Narrating familiar experience by scripture has the primary intention to instruct listeners in daily living as it relates to the life of faith. The preacher directs listeners in living a life of faith in the daily realities of human existence. This approach is almost one of discipleship through preaching. The approach is enveloped by moral and ethical dimensions, with implications of what we "ought to do." The preacher might use phrases such as "you should," "we are called to," "we learn," "we need to understand," or "the lesson we see and learn here." If a formula or equation were used to describe this approach, it would look similar to this: the scripture states = therefore, we should.

Here, a preacher may use instruction in a way that is similar to reasoning, answering, or validation, in that they both provide some form of answer. However, the difference between instruction and the process of reasoning and answering is that the answers of instruction are not necessarily grounded in the premise of explaining or giving purpose to some occurrence in daily life. The intentions in instruction are to provide guidance based on scripture, answering the questions: "what should we do?" or "how should we live?" For instance, Barbara uses the narrative of King Jehoshaphat going into battle from 2 Chronicles 20:1-23 as a mechanism to instruct listeners in what they should do "if they are against all odds":

> So, if you are a real person with real issues and need a real solution . . . let me show you a real God that can show up and show out. Let's look at the text and find out what we should do if we are against all odds.
>
> What do you do?
>
> a. Stand up!—verse 5 says, then Jehoshaphat stood up. . . . b. Stand still. / After Jehoshaphat stood up and prayed this prayer of faith . . . He [God] says [in verse 17] "you don't have to fight this battle. Take up your positions; stand firm and see the deliverance the Lord will give you."

Recovering Sacred Texts for Preaching

> . . . c. After you have stand [stood] up against the enemy and stand still in battle, it's time to start singing—verse 22, "as they began to sing and praise, the Lord set ambushes against the men of Ammon and Moab and Mount Seir . . . and they were defeated." Your praise confuses the enemy. —Barbara

Barbara offers "a real solution" to her listeners based on the desire to know what they "should do," as opposed to "why is this happening?" She then takes the listeners through a verse-by-verse exploration that uncovers the answers, instructing them to stand up, stand still, and sing as King Jehoshaphat did.

Similarly, Louise uses each character from the parable of the prodigal son in Luke 15:11-23 to teach those gathered a lesson:

> The father teaches us we should give, but never give up; the son has a message for us, "Be careful how you use it, you could lose it." —Louise

The preacher's instructions account for the community's engagement with others; she directs listeners to offer support (give) and have hope (never give up) in the ability of others to return when they have strayed from the path, just as the father of the prodigal son teaches. She also instructs the community by warning them about squandering what they have been graciously given, as the prodigal son misused and lost what he was given. The movement between the world of the text and the world of listeners directs and gives instruction for how one is called to live in the world, and scripture holds the authority over life for offering such direction.

In the available options for creating fluidity between the worlds of the text and listener, preaching maintains the greatest equilibrium between the authority of scripture and the authority of daily life when narrating familiar experience *into* scripture. In this approach, daily life experience and the text run parallel to each other, and at times they collapse into one entity. There is an almost seamless overlap between the two. The preacher uses a means of strong identification between the world and people of scripture and the world and people of their communities. She takes great liberties in expanding and narrowing the text for her community. In these liberties, the preacher demonstrates and models a comfort interacting with scripture. The objective is to show the significance of scripture in daily life, or relationship between the two, through minimizing the distance between scripture and life experiences.

When life collapses into the text, images and the conditions of the preachers' and listeners' lives suddenly appear in the narrative of scripture. For instance, Louise places her and her listener's life world into the narration of the story of the prodigal son. The preacher acknowledges what she is about to do: "Jesus does not put a name on the individuals in this text; I suppose that is so that each of us could see what it would be like to lose something that is near and dear to you." She also gives individuals permission to "see themselves" in the text, write themselves into the story of the unnamed, and then narrate their world into the text:

> The unsuspecting young man did not know that the money would run out so soon. And the economy took a nosedive and with all of the partying that he had done, there was no money and no job prospects. Living such a rich life, everything that he had was gone. Friendless, no family connections, no employment, unable to purchase new tires for the car, no money to pay the condo note, he was becoming desperate. And my friends, desperate people take desperate measures. So he went and hired himself out to a citizen of that country who sent him to feed the pigs.
> —Louise

The woes and desperation of people during the 2011 economic crisis become inseparable from the hardship and desperation of the prodigal son. Louise describes the economy taking a nosedive, job prospects running out, needing new tires for the car without having the money to pay for them, and having no money for the condo rent. The desperation of individuals in 2011 *is* the desperation of the prodigal son. She has just removed the temporal separation that could potentially exist between the text and her listeners, almost forcing their identification with the situation in scripture based on her understanding of the inner working principles of the narrative.

There are also times in preaching when we might bring biblical characters and stories into our world. This practice is an inverse of Louise's engagement with the prodigal son above. In contrast to Louise's approach, Sharon's approach brings Jesus to the steps of the church where she is preaching in order to ask the congregation a question as they enter worship:

> If Jesus stood on the steps outside of this church and asked each one of us as we enter the building "Who do you say that I am?" . . . How would our worship look? Would we act quirky, show spontaneous acts of kindness, actually say to someone come share my pew, would our giving in offerings be unpredictable, or would we cry ugly tears of joy when we sing the songs of Zion. —Sharon

In Sharon's narration, Jesus poses the question, "Who do you say that I am?" She is not narrating a random question but is utilizing the same question Jesus asks his disciples in Matthew 16:13-20, which is the scripture she chose for the sermon. Sharon brings Jesus into the real life world of her and her listeners, while those gathered now become the very disciples who are in Matthew 16:13-20. She is probing for the "real life Peter" in her midst who will say, "You are the Messiah, the son of the living God." In this way, she uses Jesus as an imminent and living being engaging the immediate life of the community.

Creating fluidity between the daily life world and the world of scripture attends to the "how" in the process of helping listeners connect with an interpretation of scripture. As the preacher makes choices about how to highlight the slippage between the world of the text and her world, she gives listeners permission to engage and interpret the significance of the text for their lives. The choices of identification, even as they engage the imagination, are simultaneously interpretative decisions. These choices may seem rudimentary or mundane; however, when one ascertains how to engage in these basic premises of narrating lived experience *out of*, *by*, and *into* scripture, she is able to build upon them for more creatively nuanced interpretive practices for the sake of "getting away with" what a community may deem a more controversial interpretive approach. One would risk the costs of engaging in a more controversial interpretation when lives would remain at stake if she takes the "safer route."

chapter 4

Meticulous Engagement and Filling out the Story

The preacher's primary concern in meticulously engaging scripture is determining to *what* material she will attend or make use of in the process of interpretation. If we understand preaching as a practice that generally attends to life when engaging scripture, be it for the means of answer or reason, instruction or discipleship, or strong identification, we can then use this understanding for the sake of a more intentional and meticulous engagement of a text. This meticulous engagement might involve coloring-in the story of scripture by attending to missing details and the often overlooked or highlighting and turning up the volume on what might seem like a small or obscure detail. Basic connections between the text and daily life world lend to more particular connections between the text and daily life world. These connections are significant when considering those aspects that connect to the particular lived experiences of the preacher and listeners.

We naturally gravitate to things that pique our interests or that which we subconsciously align or find resonance. The argument here for engaging scripture is that the preacher overtly owns those places of alignment and identification for the sake of exploration. A preacher might determine that there is a need to give careful attention to when a character is a woman, whether she is a protagonist, antagonist, or peripheral character in a narrative. And then when attending to the character the preacher would need to engage the woman, her actions, how others respond to her, and ultimately, how God interacts with her in the story. If the exploration proves worthy for preaching, there is an opportunity to disrupt unproductive and often harmful scripts.

This approach of meticulous engagement can be combined with the tools of narrating lived experience into, out of, or by scripture, as it is the process of using one's wisdom for coloring in the *what* (content) of those interpretive strategies. Here the purpose is to understand a text. The preacher places an emphasis on "getting inside of" the text and assists listeners in seeing its inner angles. The text holds the authority, in that there is something meaningful that needs to be unearthed and understood in the engagement of scripture for its own sake that will then be instrumental to the overall message. Yet that understanding never escapes a conversation with the wisdom of the preacher.

When we fill out the story, we expand the details and information beyond that which is immediately on the page. The preacher may fill out the story by unearthing historical premises about the passage and the world of scripture. She may make use of imaginative elaboration to further clarify and amplify seemingly scanty material and information. Filling out the story could closely resemble the collapse of worlds that occurs when narrating familiar experience into scripture, and is a part of how the preacher might build up to the path of her overarching message (making meaning).

The differences between collapsing the worlds of scripture and today and filling out the story reside in their objectives. The objective of understanding a text for its own sake, filling out the story, is different from the objective of showing the immediate implications and significance of a text on the daily life world, narrating familiar experience into scripture. We witness the intentions of filling out the story when information and imagination are used to "turn up the volume," or increase awareness around some aspect of scripture. The preacher might utilize information and imagination in both expansive and succinct forms.

For instance, we often use history as one way of providing additional information in order to facilitate understanding. Vicki utilizes very expansive forms of historical information in her sermon based on Mark 14:3-9 (NRSV), in order to help her listeners understand the magnitude of the sacrifice a woman made in anointing Jesus's head with expensive oil and why those watching the woman criticized her action as a frivolous misuse of money. Vicki is immediately addressing the third verse of the text, which reads "a woman came with an alabaster jar of very expensive ointment or nard, and she broke open the jar and poured the ointment on his head." In her normal pattern, Vicki pulls on the expert witness; in this sermon, the expert is Charles Long, an African American historian of religion:

> . . . Oil is used to anoint kings, dignitaries and is used in varieties of celebrations. —Vicki

chapter 4

Vicki explains that oil was used to anoint kings and dignitaries and was used in celebrations in the biblical world. She then explains why the oil the woman used was so costly and precious:

> It is not indigenous to Palestine but in fact is so costly because it is imported from the Himalayan Mountains in Nepal India. . . . [T]he distance the oil has to travel to must be calculated into the cost. . . . The distance between where the oil begins and ends its journey is over 3,700 miles. You could leave from right here in Washington, DC and travel to San Diego California and still not cover 3,700 miles. —Vicki

The oil is costly because it had to travel from India to Bethany. Though the regions of manufacturing are not a part of Vicki's passage of scripture, she uses the additional information to show how the type of oil, the distance it had to travel, and the cost of "paying the workers' time and talents" drove up the oil's final price. Vicki then continues to explain that a lengthy process called "steam distillery" was used to extract the oil, while she describes the oil's "balsamic, bitter, and spicy" fragrance. She calculates the cost of pure nard in its one-ounce, eight-ounce, and thirty-two-ounce packaging. And only then does the preacher return to the initial words of scripture that evoked the "filling out":

> It is this costly ointment this woman in Mark is bringing to Jesus as oil for the pouring. —Vicki

The preacher used all of the additional information in order to explain the cost of the oil, for the purpose of helping listeners understand the woman's actions and the surrounding controversy. Understanding the cost of the oil is of real importance to Vicki's later claims about the passage; therefore, her listeners need more insight about the costliness of the oil the woman offers as it will eventually relate to the costliness of the sacrifice they are being called to make. For Vicki, without understanding the internal dynamics of scripture, one cannot understand the major claims scripture has on our lives.

Just as Vicki uses a great amount of historical and external information in order to promote understanding, Sharon uses a more succinct form of illustrative elaboration to do so. Sharon describes John 8:1-11 and narrates the story of "the church folk" bringing a "nameless woman," supposedly caught in the "very act of adultery," before Jesus and "into the hearing of all the people that were gathered." She immediately replaces the original presence of the "Scribes and Pharisees" as instigators with "church folk" who are equally intrusive. She draws attention to the fact that the writer did not "name" the woman but called her a "nameless woman." Sharon has now set the stage for understanding the woman as being thought of as an insignificant pawn in the hands of those who were religious.

Sharon then uses imaginative elaboration to help listeners understand the "shame" and "dehumanization" of the event, as the woman was brought before Jesus as he wrote silently in the dust:

> Jesus said nothing. Can you imagine being in the place of this woman, your clothes hanging off, your embarrassed, shame-faced tears running down and you hear the grasps [gasps] of the people surrounded? And Jesus said nothing. —Sharon

As she imagines and fills out the story, describing the woman's teary, ashamed face, and hanging clothes, she asks her listeners to engage their imaginations as well:

> This dehumanized woman pushed to the ground to only stare at and smell the dirty feet of her accusers and now in the presence of the king of Kings and Lord of Lords, waiting for His verdict and he said nothing. —Sharon

She places the woman on the ground staring at and smelling dirty feet before she moves back to addressing Jesus's silence. The information Sharon provides is not a part of the passage but serves as a means for filling out the emotional gaps of the woman's story, which exist between the leaders questioning Jesus about her fate and Jesus's actions of drawing in the sand. As she fills out scripture's narrative, Sharon's choosing to meticulously treat the scanty character development of the nameless woman is noteworthy, as the woman only has one line of speech that is limited to three words. When we choose to focus on the relationships within scripture by intentionally directing attention to particular characters in the story and providing narrative details that are not on the page, our experience of the text comes to the forefront.

There is possibility in (re)imagining this practice of filling out the story as an intentional tool of creativity. These preachers make use of the traditions of identification and filling out the story, all while having a distinct leaning toward the periphery of the passage and the feminine experience in the narrative. They use the tradition's tools that are at their disposal, while they unapologetically connect experience—often their own—with their engagement with scripture. They demonstrate a proclivity and the potential present in giving scripture detailed attention when a female protagonist or antagonist is involved, especially when the text presents a "a tough situation." Their meticulous engagement of scripture does not exclude filling out the story but now meets filling out the story with very intentional content.

For instance, in Sharon's sermon above, in which she fills in the absent emotions of the woman, she also introduces other "scandalous women" into the narrative of scripture via Jesus's subconscious and actions:

> Bowed down Jesus looks at the woman in her shame, and feels her pain and he begins to write in the dust of the ground. We are not told what he wrote but maybe he wrote—
>
> "Grandmother Ruth, went into Boaz' place and uncovered his feet at night."
>
> "My cousin, Rahab was a prostitute."
>
> "My mother, Mary, became pregnant before marriage and had the death sentence to be stoned placed on her."
>
> I wonder if Jesus remembered his Aunt Tamar . . . the daughter of King David [who] was raped in the king's palace. —Sharon

Jesus is now writing the names of women from his genealogy into the sand—women who could be questioned about their own bodily engagements. The preacher brings Jesus, Ruth, Rahab, Mary, and Tamar to the defense of this woman's shame and as counter witnesses to the religious leaders' accusations. The preacher sifts through the genealogy of Jesus and the portraits of women in scripture in order to create an understanding around the shame, dehumanization, and injustices in the passage.

Sharon's remaining in the mode of narrator without expressing any present-day implications is of real importance; she helps listeners see a more complex angle of scripture as she gets inside of the phenomena of the passage. While Sharon excavates the primary narrative of the text—Jesus and the woman before him—she excavates the past narratives of women in scripture, including Ruth, Rahab, Mary, and Tamar. She invites the alliances of other biblical women into the story as she narrates the conscience of Jesus. She fills in the story as black preaching traditions entail, but she fills out the story around the female character, instead of around the teaching of Jesus and the religious leaders who accuse her—all of whom have the most explicit roles in the narrative. For Sharon, identification takes shape in listeners' identifying with the woman's shame, humiliation, undue treatment, and a story that is not isolated to her own.

In contexts that remain male preferential, women characters are often easily ignored or portrayed in ways that are commensurate with negative tropes of womanhood, which the texts of scripture do not escape. Such negative tropes about black womanhood continue to trace along several scripts. For instance, the script of the-strong-black-woman is the assumption that black women possess supernatural strength and power to face and overcome life's trials.[6] There are scripts that view black women's bodies and actions as sinful, untrustworthy, and oversexed—meaning they have an excessive sexual appetite—and others can be easily excused for their use of black women as sexual objects. And lastly, some assume an untrustworthy *nature* corresponds equally to black women, which lends to their need to be watched and monitored by men and whiteness in this line of rationale.

Living in a world in which women are inherently distrusted and not valued as sources of truth makes the way in which we approach scripture and its intersection with the lives of women particularly significant. When attending to texts that involve women characters (or allusions to the feminine),[7] the preacher needs to rely on creative intelligence and a collective lived wisdom, which in their best instances support thriving and wellbeing. When black women use what they know about living in a world that does not privilege their existence as a lens to engage a text, this is the means by which they might simultaneously (re)cast understandings of women in scripture and the understanding of women, particularly black women, in the contemporary world.

Preaching against the Text

The preacher must determine how to narrate the parallels between the ancient world and contemporary world, through a reimagining that collapses, amplifies, or directs listeners toward the intersections of the two. The fluidity present in these encounters between the worlds is not to be dismissed or underestimated, especially when black women preach. The preacher facilitates the abilities of listeners to own their freedom to encounter and even question scripture, as she creates points of connection among texts, the contemporary world, and listeners. In turn, the preacher brings listeners closer to the questions and experiences of everyday life and how those experiences and their wisdom intersect with the text at hand. As the preacher renders a text and its exploration accessible to listeners through identification, she also opens up the possibility of using a text to undo itself while not undermining the authority scripture holds within a community. For the preacher has not discarded scripture but moves toward her final interpretation through a meticulous engagement of a text.

In many cases this must be the work of black women in preaching, particularly as we preach texts that have been overtly or subtly used for our subjugation to second class or non-personhood. Because the hope is to bring the community along in the discovery of truth, how to go about the task and what material is used when creating touch points with scripture are just as important as final interpretive decisions. And for the preaching of black women the *how* and *what* are extremely significant when their articulations of truth loom under the shadows of contestation, or may read against what the community has previously accepted as valid interpretations of scripture.

In Vicki's sermon "The Silence We Keep," we see a window into using experience to refute and correct the content of scripture as it simultaneously shows how the engagement with lived experience and scripture continue to coexist. Vicki preaches from 2 Samuel 13:19-20 (NRSV), where the rape of Tamar by her brother Amnon is recounted. After being raped, Tamar is told by her brother Absalom: "Be quiet for now, my sister; he is your brother. Don't take this thing to heart." The resolution in the immediate narrative of scripture is that neither Tamar's father, King David, nor her brother Absalom confronts her brother and rapist Amnon in their knowledge of the violence against her. Instead, both father and brother remain silent in a greater allegiance to the household and family.

Vicki first uses scripture as a mirror for the support and validation of what happens in life as scripture demonstrates her community's tendencies in daily life. The preacher's interpretation is grounded in her and the community's experiences of sexual abuse:

> Just like our sister Tamar, we have a tendency to devalue our existence by keeping silent about childhood sexual abuses we have suffered, in order to avoid exposing our families to public humiliation. As African Americans we place greater value on the opinions of those we love as an entity, as opposed to the individuals who constitute our "skin and kin." —Vicki[8]

Vicki implicates both the survivors of sexual abuse for their silence and the community for its complacency and role in valuing solidarity over individual sanctity. Even as I am attentive to my personal rejection of implicating survivors of sexual abuse, I cannot overlook and not give attention to the ingenuity present in Vicki's interpretative strategies for the sake of gaining a listening. In this sermon, Tamar's story becomes subsumed by the stories of those within the preacher's community, to the point of identifying the story of Tamar as their story. And then the preacher bears witness to why the narrative cannot hold authority to repeat itself in the life of the immediate community. Vicki calls forth the narratives of family and community secrets in the black struggle to survive, the experiences of victims and survivors of sexual abuse, and the voices of black women. She uses an approach of identification and then moves to using juxtaposition, as she deems the resolution in scripture troublesome and undesirable:

> Tamar lived in patriarchal times and within a situation of life far different from our lives today. Our response to sexual violence within our family does not have to be the same as hers. Dr. Valerie Bridgeman Davis suggests that while "it is unfortunate that Tamar's community forced her to carry the guilt and shame and forced her to live her life as a desolate woman living in her brother Absalom's house," that does not have to be our present reality. As the virgin daughter of the King, her options were limited yet as honored and beloved daughter(s) of THE KING our options can be far different. —Vicki

Using the voice of the "expert," Hebrew Bible scholar Valerie Bridgeman, the preacher claims that the resolution to rape and violence in the narrative of scripture does not have to be the resolution to rape and violence in our lives today. She articulates that our "options" today, as "honored and beloved daughters" of God, are not as limited as Tamar's options were as a "virgin daughter of the king." In this instance, Vicki does not want scripture to be modeled in daily life; instead, she wants the actions of her community to correct both the undesirable aspects of scripture and the undesirable in its midst:

> If we continue in this way, generations of our kindred will suffer wounds of the heart and mind that the body cannot easily expel. Our communities and households will continue to lose its great thinkers, dreamers, preachers, artists, daughters and sons because of the psychological and spiritual damage inflicted upon them. . . . If we do not change the dysfunctional course we have embarked upon perpetrators will be free to abuse more children; the cycle of violence, unchecked, will continue and millions of our clan and tribe will suffer in silence. —Vicki

For Vicki, following the resolution in scripture's narrative has consequences too great within her community. Instead, she calls listeners to recognize the tragedy of this end in the biblical story, and not to replicate it in their community. For, if they continue to keep as silent as Tamar, David, and Absalom, the "kindred will suffer." In this instance, she envisions life and faith in God as something different from that which scripture delineates. Vicki places scripture in subordination to experience; however, in the end, she puts both scripture and the present-day actions of her community in subordination of a yet to be achieved, but desirable, resolution to end silence around sexual violence. Ultimately, the preacher's claims rest in the authority of her larger theological understandings. The preacher is making a bold move and claims faith's authority over both her community's experience thus far and scripture.

The preacher's main premise is that to give Tamar's narrative, as written, prescriptive authority within the community makes the entire community complicit in its own suffering and the suffering of individuals. In being complicit in such suffering, the community moves further away from the vision of God. Scripture continues to hold value in her attending to it, as opposed to leaving it unattended; however, the preacher's understanding of life with faith and God also allows her to subjugate the authority of scripture to her God-talk (which will be further discussed in chapter 5). For Vicki, yes, scripture is valuable but not valuable enough to put the well-being of her community or the understanding of God's vision at risk.

Considering the central role of scripture in black preaching traditions—and, by inference, within black faith communities—Vicki engages and deploys a risky interpretation of scripture. Ironically, the tradition that allows the Bible to be *my story* also allows the story to be expanded. The tradition makes room for scripture to be encountered by the particulars of the story; including the subjectivities of black, woman, and sexual-abuse survivor. Therefore, as the preacher bears witness to her encounter of scripture, her interpretation arises as one that both is significant and bears authority. Vicki's interpretation of scripture is influenced by the ways in which she makes entry into the text based on experience and by her understanding of God's vision. In short, the preacher's core faith values that attend to freedom and well-being direct her engagement with scripture, but they are further supported by the tradition's strong identification with the biblical story. She makes use of the tradition to preach against the text.

chapter 4

Ingenuity and Interpreting Scripture

The preacher who seeks thriving for all in a community's context is attentive to not drawing false equivalences or un-interrogated implications from the texts of scripture, especially texts that potentially place real lives and bodies at risk. Just as the contemporary world is fraught with dynamics of power, displacement, personal trauma, and communal hopes and sorrow, so too are the stories of the ancient worlds that scripture propels forward. The contemporary preacher wrestles with a tradition's historical interpretation of these dynamics within sacred texts, the lives of people in ancient times, and the dynamics with which her world is fraught. Scripture, its interpretation, and preaching continue forward in contemporary contexts for the sake of ringing true and being accountable to life in the present-day world.

When black women own scripture within their communities as *our story* there is the potential to interrupt and expose the ways in which the community's traditions of interpreting texts have excluded the lived wisdom and experiences of black women. Those exclusionary practices have implicitly stated to black women, "Scripture is not your story." The corrective to these interpretive failures is a reversal of roles, in such a way that scripture is the story of black women. If scripture cannot be the story of black women, it cannot be a story for the community in which black women exist. When a preacher claims her vibrant subjectivity as she engages in play and interplay with a text, she claims: "Scripture is *my story* and *our story*." And in turn, interpretations of scripture hold the possibility to more fully reflect the multiplicity of experiences in a community.

Women have a history of interpretive practices with scripture that attend to the multiplicity of experiences. Carol Norén classifies two distinct starting places of interpretation that have framed preaching women's encounters with the Bible—namely those that have theological and political trajectories and those that have social and psychological trajectories.[9] Within the theological and political framework, the preacher is prone to look at familiar texts but emphasize aspects of the story that are usually left unattended, which includes having the preacher and listeners identify with characters with whom they would not normally identify.[10] Thus, the preacher is more likely to favor narrative texts over didactic texts. The preacher seeks an account of God's action in history as opposed to long-standing laws, while being prone to assume that the community has a responsibility to "move towards God's new social order, to work for it, to announce it, and train for it."[11] In the social and psychological framework, the preacher usually attends to the least powerful characters and is more likely to amplify the biblical story by retelling it through a line-by-line exposition or making concrete analogies between the story of the text and that of the present.[12]

The emphasis on subjectivity within both black and women's preaching traditions creates affinities between the two traditions, while the sermons these preaching women offer press the expansion of both, in so far as their practices retain women's and black experiences as simultaneously significant. With this in mind, a fuller expression of scripture as *my story* makes room for the ability to connect with the text in ways that limit barriers between black women and their lives as lenses of interpretation. The work of biblical scholarship that intentionally engages the lived experiences of black women aids in strategically supporting these ongoing practices of interpretation. Mitzi J. Smith describes the project of womanist biblical interpretation as "audaciously" starting with concerning oneself with the lives of black women and their communities;[13] this audacious starting point prioritizes the particular and communal "lived experiences, history, and artifacts of black women and other women of color as a point of departure, focal point, and an overarching interpretive lens for critical analysis of the Bible and other sacred texts, contexts, cultures, readers, and readings."[14]

Preaching traditions are known for their ability to place the biblical stories alongside being human and attempting to make sense of life. This movement between the biblical and contemporary worlds assumes a connection with the text and assumes its accessibility. Because of the pull-push for accountability to today, the approach to interpreting scripture is not one of science and rationale alone but one that leaves room for intuiting and imagining these connections alongside the preacher's lived wisdom. Placing this lived wisdom in conversation with tools and resources that support instead of limit the processes of imagination and intuition is the fulcrum for resourcing the ingenuity already at work in black women's practices of interpreting scripture for preaching. Furthermore, for those who are not black women, expanding your resources for interpretation will assist in your use of scripture for the sake of an organic word that promotes life over death for the lives of black women.

To be clear, the ability of black women to engage scripture with an intimate interpretive authority opens the text up anew for the entire community—providing an alternative engagement with scripture by the community. For instance, when black women preach, the community might experience the ability to listen anew to the stories of Delilah and Samson, Bat-Jephthah (Jepthah's daughter), the unnamed dismembered woman of Judges 19, Queen Vashti, and young Hadassah who was groomed to become Queen Esther. Interpretations of these texts when placed alongside the lived experiences of black women in the contemporary world may afford these women to be (re)cast as the center of their stories. (Re)casting these women moves them beyond the gaze of their male exploiters, abusers, and perpetrators, which has often materialized in interpretations that end with moralistic claims that implicitly or explicitly support the continual practice of rendering bodies of difference invisible.

(Re)Imagining Sermon Development

If a preacher seeks to both use and repurpose interpretive approaches for preaching, they must (re)imagine their approach to the text in sermon development. Such (re)imagining does not constrain or forbid the process of bringing the preacher and their community to the text at its first encounter but relies on the presence of the experiences of preacher and community at the first encounter of scripture. As the preacher begins with experience from the outset, they begin discerning right-fitting and meaningful possibilities of valid interpretations of scripture that honor the porous boundaries in the distinction between an ancient world and the world in which they lives. This interaction with scripture for preaching is an experiential one.

When both life and scripture hold authority, the preacher may assume freedom in their encounter of a text. At first, scripture may be a distant text of a foreign world, which appears inaccessible. However, the preacher's knowledge of life—what it means to be human in the world and to live as a person of faith—removes the first barriers to both engaging scripture and interpreting its significance for the community. Scripture is accessible to us, and lived experience shrinks the gap between the ancient and contemporary worlds.

The sermon makes evident a preacher's final interpretive decisions. And through the sermon we offer our encounter of the text, as a bridge that affords listeners the possibility of freely encountering the text with us. The shared encounter of a text through preaching makes possible a buildup toward shared and agreed-upon meanings of scripture. In preaching we help listeners experience the reflections of truth we experienced in scripture. However, the *Amen* moment only occurs when the listeners and preacher together experience an alignment of what they each consider a valid interpretation of scripture—that is, shared meaning. Therefore, the preacher's work is to create points of connection between scripture and the lives of listeners in such a way that the message might be received.

Learning this approach to preaching relies on the preacher's ability to pursue a new or enlivened encounter of scripture. For a fresh encounter with scripture draws the community out of its "memory" of the passage alone, while making way for an immediate experience that is relevant to the ongoing realities of life at hand. This encounter is facilitated through points of resonation between the text and life and requires the preacher first to move *beyond memory to immediate encounter* in the very process of sermon development. Activating the body, or *embodying the text*, while engaging the biblical text is a significant factor in facilitating this immediate encounter. Embodiment is the way in which we engage the world around us, and sensory aspects are central to how we approach the text, including imagery, sounds, and emotions. A preacher's ability to engage scripture as a sensory encounter creates another opportunity to minimize the boundaries between familiar experience and scripture—as they are not afraid to make play on the boundaries that exist between the text and life today.

chapter 4

The ability to play with the fluidity between the language and content of the text and between the language and experiences of today helps the preacher locate further points of connection with scripture. *Contemporary play on scripture* is crucial for the preacher to access their elusive understanding of the contemporary meaning and value of the text. However, in this mode of play, the preacher must make every attempt to experience the otherness of the text also—the ways it might "push back" against our experience or how our experiences might "push back" against the text. This experimentation between the push and pull of the text and what one knows about life today, is where the preacher begins making decisions about preaching with or against the current of the text. And whatever that final decision may be, the preacher strives to understand the text within its larger tradition of interpretation. Here, they explore some of the limits and possibilities of scripture within the larger community, through the process of *tracking down the text*.

We are able to facilitate an experience of scripture in as far as we ourselves engage in an experience in which neither scripture nor experience stand alone but function in close proximity to one another. As an individual encounters, embodies, makes play with, and tracks down a text, the imagination is continually engaged in the process of determining and conveying a message.

Beyond Memory to Immediate Encounter

Preaching for the sake of life, which retains life and scripture as authoritative, assumes a type of immediacy or imminence even in the way we interpret a text. This immediacy draws listeners out of their memory and out of the process of replaying memorized tapes about biblical passages in their minds. At the same time, this encounter with the biblical text helps to focus the sermon on a present (in the room) message, while simultaneously inviting a new experience of something that could be very familiar—namely, scripture. A preacher's imagination and imaginative engagement with the text is the crux of engaging scripture in a way that moves beyond memory to immediate encounter. The preacher is intentional about actively attending to the imagination in this way of engaging scripture.

Engaging the imagination as a significant resource for preaching is not a new phenomenon;[15] yet, the imagination is what is left behind often and considered not serious enough for the weighty task of preaching. The imagination is the resource that allows the preacher to unlock what lies within both themselves and the text. This process of revealing includes the meanings we derive through engaging scripture. We literally find our way to that which we intuit but cannot yet articulate or conceptualize as we manipulate that which we can perceive, allowing the imagination to reveal more.

The imagination is an intellectual faculty based on our entire way of intuiting, knowing, and moving about the world. Our imagination is what enables us to find alignment between things that might not readily align otherwise, and sometimes for the sake of envisioning a possibility we have yet to experience. This intelligible compass allows us to move between a present reality that we know and a future or past reality we may or may not have experienced before. For the sake of preaching, the preacher engages their imagination for the purposes of meeting the imagination of listeners in the preaching moment.

The hope is for the preacher to practice imaginative engagement through the sermon development process. This approach is in contrast to suppressing the imagination and using it as an *ad hoc* at the end of sermon preparation. Allowing the imagination to saturate all stages of sermon development includes our initial engagement with scripture. Through the imagination we offer depth, cast insight, and amplify texts, creating an experience of scripture that is new and enlivened.

The preacher's intentional focus on a *fresh reading* or immediate-prolonged encounter with a text helps move the preacher beyond memory, while connecting and making room for imaginative thoughts and play. Anna Carter Florence describes this up-close and personal encounter with scripture as "living in a text," in which a preacher attends to the text by describing and testifying to what they see as they remain open and spend time with a passage of scripture.[16] This engagement with scripture is a slow and intentional process facilitated by openness to both the text and the imagination. Furthermore, this is the place in sermon development where the preacher first gives their voice—as in judgments, intuitions, and reasoning—permission to enter the process. At some point, yes, the fruits of imaginative labor must be ordered and carefully arranged;[17] the preacher needs to determine how to collect their thoughts for the sermon, including what to leave behind. But not at this stage in sermon development. Going to the "orderly process" too soon will preempt sermonic possibilities that arise first and foremost from the preacher's own deepest ways of knowing and intuiting.

The greatest hurdle for many preachers, especially those who have had their judgments and voices second guessed in life in general and in the pulpit in particular, is allowing the imagination to run freely; this will feel like one of the most uncomfortable and challenging tasks in sermon development. The preacher is challenged in new territory—that of trusting her intuition, opening up, and freefalling. We are prone to actively resist the silence cultivated by the need of "getting it right" or the self-doubt of "you don't know." In truth, we do not yet know the outcome; and therefore, there are no right or wrong responses at this stage. This is the stage in every class where I scream from the middle of the floor "Sin! And sin boldly!"

The goal here is to move beyond memory to immediate encounter, to begin an encounter with the passage not previously had, to track down what stands out at a particular time, and to begin to make the sensory connections that are more fully explored below in embodying the text.

IN PRACTICE
Beyond Memory to Immediate Encounter

Here are some practical steps to help move outward from the memory of a text and into a space in which you are open to an immediate encounter of a text:

1. Print out an enlarged version of the passage. At every juncture, feel free to "mark up" the page and color code similar words, images, or references.

2. Read the text as if it is not familiar. Try reading the passage slowly, trying to restrain the tendency to fill in the story from memory.

3. Now, read the passage aloud, or consider having someone else read it aloud, and listen to it. If it is a narrative text, have different individuals take on the voices of different characters.

4. Jot down the first thoughts that come to your mind. Note words that are similar or evoke similar ideas, images, or meaning.

5. List all of the characters present (both major and minor). Describe the personal characteristics of the characters.

6. List the imagery present in the text (i.e., rocky roads, dirt roads, streams, city, fire, etc.).

• •

Pausing and lingering with the text is a stumbling block both for those who need to build the muscles of trusting their voices and for those who have had their voices often affirmed. In the classroom, during exercises of encounter I literally see words *tremor* at the edge of lips threatening to come forth and then sucked back down into silence by uncertainty, self-editing, and the threat of the thought of being too risky or simple and dismissed. This is also the moment in the process where the know-it-all comes to the text already having the answers and resolute about what the sermon will be, or they just cannot resist showing off what they "know" about the significance of a symbol in the passage. Even this "charging forth" in certainty is a hiding of one's deepest voice and shrouding vulnerability. Allowing oneself to freely encounter the text holds the greatest possibility for discovering an utterance that both apprehends the preacher and listeners as it rings in the possibilities of truth for here and now.

Embodying the Text

In an experiential engagement of scripture, we rely on the ability to make sensory connections between the biblical world and contemporary settings, further collapsing the boundaries between the two. This sensory connection is of importance because it helps listeners connect their experiences with the scripture and vice versa; and it helps scripture become a dynamic reality in the midst of the community as opposed to a static and received text. Sensory aspects of touch, taste, smell, hearing, sight, and feeling are the means by which we often fill out or fill in the emotions, sounds, and voices evoked by scripture.

The body is the medium of all that is sensory. Therefore, embodying scripture is one means of moving the text away from existing as an abstract and distant entity to something that possesses lively properties and possibilities, helping the preacher make additional concrete connections between scripture and human experience. The preacher's ability to engage the sensorium while engaging scripture mediates the biblical text through the body, making it a text encountered by a body that will connect with the everyday experiences of bodies. Workshopping the text through the body allows for an exchange between the preacher and text in close proximity, as scripture comes through and acts upon the body, engaging the senses. The preacher approaches the text not as something to be thought about but rather as an experience to be had, as the preacher allows their full self to be engaged and acted upon by the text.[18]

Anna Carter Florence notes that the sensory approach to scripture limits the tendency to "think about" or "talk about" a text, which places distance between the text and preacher;[19] instead, "it is about *what we saw and heard in the text* when we engaged it deeply; it is about the view seen from the vantage point of experience."[20] Distance limits a preacher's experience of a text and makes the text become an object of study. As the text becomes an "out there" object of study, the preacher is more concerned about using the right tools to unearth and excavate the true and objective meaning of a passage (i.e., including lexicons, commentaries, and original language). Embodying scripture literally removes the literal distance in space between scripture and the body.

As we remove the distance between ourselves and scripture, the process creates an experience through our vulnerability. As the preacher dwells in the text, they model the encounter they hope to facilitate for listeners as one describes what they have seen and heard in their own encounter with scripture.[21] Ultimately, this encounter is the message we offer and seek to describe in preaching. The greatest obstacle in this process is the preacher and the extent to which they will or will not limit the distance between the text and self. This removal of distance happens in multiple ways. If our bodies have been limited and constrained in our everyday lives—including how we move about in the world and how we show up and are presented or dressed—embodying the text is a means of making sensory connections with the text. However, it is also a way for the preacher who may have had distanced or highly regimented relationship to their body to become at home or more comfortable in their body as the medium for preaching.

IN PRACTICE
Embodying the Text

Here are some practical steps to help workshop a passage of scripture through the body:

1. Read aloud, listen to, or sign the passage, as applicable. Each time you go through the text, engage the text through a different part of the sensorium: touch, taste, sight, hearing, feelings, emotions, or smell.

2. What else do you experience in the text by engaging your body in this way?

3. Read, sign, or listen to the passage a third time and pay attention to bodies: Who speaks, to whom is spoken, who is spoken about, and who doesn't speak at all?

4. Make notes regarding the sensorium (touch, taste, smell, sight, hearing, emotions) experienced while reading the passage.

Embodying the text helps us connect the performances within the text to the bodily performance and experience of the text as it will be encountered by listeners. Based on our own experience, we are able to begin the process of brainstorming how we might recreate this sensory experience as we help facilitate an encounter with scripture through the sermon.

The hope is to begin with an understanding that preaching takes shape through the body and lands upon bodies within the community.

Contemporary Play with Scripture

The preacher is positioned at the meeting of three roads—traditions, present day, and ancient worlds—while attempting to forge a fourth road from that intersection. The fourth road is the sermon, fashioned by the vantage point of the one who imagines it into being—that is, the preacher. The sermon is the result of our abilities to imagine the text anew as we illuminate the moments of interplay between the text and today. In order to locate these places of interplay, the preacher might engage in literal play with scripture in both the process of sermon development and the sermon itself.

Engaging scripture with a type of play relies on an understanding that homiletical imagination for the sake of life is privileged over the hopes of ancient texts in their contexts alone. This does not mean that scripture and its historical contexts are not accounted for in preaching. And often, quite the contrary is true, especially when a text and its surface reading create stumbling blocks for the ongoing lived religious experiences of people. Literal play involves flirting with ideas, flights of fancy, and a willingness to engage an ever-evolving imagination that makes connections where they might not otherwise be made. In this play, as previously stated, there are not yet any right or wrong hunches because the preacher is in search of the possibilities.

Possibilities are discovered, almost stumbled upon. They pique our interest and curiosity while opening up new paths that push us closer to the precision we seek in naming the connection or dissonance that exists between ancient worlds and our world. These points of contact with scripture make possible the discovery of meaningful connections with the lives of listeners. The parameters of play and interplay remain simultaneously tethered to both the worlds of the text and the world of the preacher. In this process we use our creative license, which involves taking risks and liberties for the sake of making connections and illuminating understanding.

Making contemporary play with scripture *is* our owning the Bible as *our story and my story* in an openly biased way, as we seek connections for preaching. These connections move beyond what the Bible states, to how the biblical story is imagined, and finally to saying something and having import for the present day. As a text, the Bible may state but never say; to say is a product of interpretation because as soon as we move beyond stating what is on the page, we are already engaging in the act of interpretation.[22] And interpretation itself does not take place in a social or cultural vacuum. Making contemporary play actively calls forth aspects of the culturally imagined import of scripture, which is already latent in our engagement of reading the text. As we approach scripture, we are never capable of removing our own experiences from that encounter or the text or from our imagining of connections within the text. Therefore, the alternative to assuming a faux objectivist standpoint is to acknowledge our imagination and experiences from the outset by fully incorporating and acknowledging them during the process. This acknowledgement includes bringing to our engagement with scripture what Tisdale describes as the community's folk language, thus allowing our social and cultural influences to make play *on* and *with* an ancient text. In short, we must account for our biases and assumptions when interacting with a text, but not with the intention of completely discarding them.

We ultimately have to find words where words do not yet exist, for the purpose of sharing words through a sermon that does not yet exist. An aspect of making contemporary play with scripture is stumbling upon the most right-fitting connections and words, as we make way for what we most believe to be *a word from the Lord that means something for me today.* Play is the process by which we begin making meaningful connections with and confessions of belief about the text.

An inscription is a form of contemporary play with scripture. Inscription is anything that attempts to etch out the passage in a different form (for instance, drawing, speaking, painting, singing, writing, paraphrasing, or creating poetry). Inscription and description are connected entities. Anna Carter Florence explains that in giving words we bear witness not only to what we have seen and experienced in a text but also to what we believe. She states:

> "Description" is the art of writing down and writing-upon, so that others can see and understand our words. We can describe an object that exists or an image that does not exist. . . . If we are good at it we can help our listeners see and hear what we describe. . . . Whatever we describe to others about a text, whatever we try to say about it, is first de-scribed for them in us, through our engagement with that text—*because engagement leaves its own marks* . . . An honest description comes from deep engagement that could easily have been otherwise if the preacher let fear and absolutes read the day.[23]

When paraphrasing, aspects of a passage are often left out or pushed into the background. Rather than "preaching the paraphrase," preachers must examine it for the additional meanings that are in the content pushed aside during paraphrastic inscription, exploring both the absent and present content for the sermon's message. Was content pushed aside because you did not remember it? because you did not think it had much meaning in the passage? or because you just did not like it? Similarly, did you keep content because in earnest that is what you were drawn to over and over again? because it was a recurring image or word? or because for you, this is the key that unlocks the door? Inscription conceals content at the same time that it reveals content.

We are able to make our way toward various inscriptions as we see the text as a malleable or moving object with multiple angles and vantage points on which we can riff. We might approach examining a text through roaming about: exploring the different rooms, hiding behind the couch and peering outward for a different glance, and even rearranging the furniture a bit to see how it changes the atmosphere of a text. For instance, if you read a character's voice as angry the first time, what happens if you read the voice with sentiments of fear this time? What happens if you take the character whom you read as the least important character and make them the most important character of the narrative? What changes if you think about the nonhuman characters and objects? What changes if you name the nameless person in the text? This is the type of purposeful play that makes way for discovering the locales of interplay between the contemporary world and ancient texts, and even for pushing the boundaries of interpretation.

In the classroom I ask students to tell the text as a story, do a spoken word piece, rewrite it, envision the actual characters and locations, and name what they want the text to "say" and what they do not want it to "say" under any circumstance. These steps help the preacher own their inclinations toward the text and then account for them as they continue to search for the right-fitting word for today.

IN PRACTICE
Contemporary Play with Scripture

Here are some practical steps to help workshop a passage on the way to contemporary play.

1. Identify where you locate the biblical story in today's story (including its sounds, characters, textures, and emotions).

2. Are there points of similarity and dissimilarity between the text and today's world?

3. Where do you connect or disconnect with what is occurring in the text?

4. Where do you agree or disagree with what is taking place in the scripture based on your experience?

5. Is there anything that gives you pause or reservation based on your experience?

6. Create a paraphrase of the text based on what you have discovered through encountering, embodying, and naming points of identification.

7. What aspects of the passage remain present and significant, and what aspects completely disappear from the paraphrase? Explore this absent and present content for a sermon message.

As we etch and re-etch our experience of the written text, we inevitably portray our innermost beliefs, convictions, and experiences of scripture. Making contemporary play on scripture helps us discover our convictions about the passage, words for describing that conviction, and words for helping others experience scripture. In contemporary play, the hope is that inscription meets cultural influence, while keeping the text and contemporary world in direct conversation.

Preaching Against the Text

In preaching we use knowledge about life as a means to demonstrate the similarities between the text and everyday life; the import of scripture on everyday life; and, on some occasions, the ways in which the written text cannot be a sacred or honored story within our communities. In practice, we have long opened up possibilities for interpreting scripture. People of faith have figured out how to reject principles of slavery; women who preach have determined ways around the principles of women's silence; as we worship in polyester and cotton blend clothing and indulge in shrimp cocktail, we have managed to throw out Levitical codes of attire and food; and we have often mediated texts related to divorce. Here in these instances, the priority entails engaging scripture but not at the expense of sustaining life. We are willing to probe a text with deeper questions when there is a vested interested or something at stake. The problem lies in where we have drawn lines in the communal sands about who's life is or is not at stake, or for whom these questions are worth pursuing and for whom they are not.

In order to attend to the trouble and often the horrors of a text, a preacher needs to consider a few things. One needs to raise the questions begging to be asked in the text, even if their bidding is not overtly recognizable by the gathered community. And then the preacher has to determine how to raise those questions in such a way that they seem to mimic or become the voices of listeners as the sermon unfolds. In one sense, the preacher is attending to the questions begging to be asked, lying dormant within listeners, as the preacher is simultaneously turning up the volume on those questions by bringing them front and center. In preaching we may accomplish this by attending to what is blatantly in the words of a text, or we may also do this by reading between the lines, the voids, and the places where things are absent from text.

I have commonly found that the "silence" of a text is the foil for avoiding an interpretation that would do more damage than good within a community. For instance, maybe God is silent in the text and did not intervene to prevent trouble, and maybe God's silence is the lack of God's affirmation of what has taken place. Does it make the tragedy okay? No. But it also does not require us to perpetuate an image of a God who condones and loves the suffering of humanity. In a different instance, maybe humanity was silent in the text and did not intervene in action, and maybe the silence is the exemplar of what not to do. And it could be the complete reversal of both; maybe God or humanity intervened and acted in ways that inflicted harm, that create unease for the reader, or that might rightly create unease for listeners if they are not inoculated to what should be troubling. The preacher's work is to help listeners tap into what lies dormant within them: the capacity to question, consider, and probe deeper when what they know of life is upended or confronted by the traditions of scripture and belief. In these interpretive decisions the humanity within the text reaches out and touches what it means to be human in our world. This work requires the preacher to build upon the imaginative play that they have already used in conversation with scripture; however, now she explores for the possibilities of silence, voids, and making deeper connections where they might not readily exist.

In order to read against a text or preach against a text, one has to avoid the inclination to make tidy resolutions for tensions in a text for which there may not be a resolution at all. The preacher also needs to finish out the possible end of the story or what would be the end of the story for every possible "reason" or "rationale" she would want to give for the tensions in the text. Because the end of the story or the potential end of the story will land upon bodies in today's world. For instance, if we read God as the character of the text who brought about suffering and horror in the lives of people, then somehow we must consider finishing out that story line and its implications for today. And the question becomes, do

chapter 4

we think interpreting texts in a consistent manner that shows God as one who condones our suffering is sustaining to the lives or attention of the suffering people in our community? The answer would certainly be no. And in this case, the preacher has to determine how to attend deeply to the text, even while rejecting any surface level or a face value reading of the text that lacks nuance.

....

IN PRACTICE
Preaching against the Text

Here are some practical helps for exploring whether or not this may be a time to preach against the "obvious" meaning of a text:

1. In your process of encountering and making play with the text was there anything that unsettled you (i.e., a troublesome outcome, a view of God you did not like, a view of humanity that was disturbing)?

2. Are there any deep places of sadness or outrage in the text?

3. What does not add up or make sense about the text?

4. Is there something to which you are asking the question, "Why this way?" or were you thinking, "This did not have to happen?"

5. Where is God in the text? Where do you think God is *not* in the text?

6. Is there any possibility that what you hope to be the best possible truth about God is present in a character in the text?

7. Is there something that you know about the world and life today that makes this passage difficult to preach, or that you think could cause harm to someone if it is preached?

....

In truth we may decide that a portion of a text cannot be held up as a word that sustains life, or the entirety of a passage undermines life in our midst. There are times when we are called to remind listeners that the "good news" is not celebratory news at all; instead God makes way and space for lament and our crying out about what is not yet as it should be.

Tracking Down the Text

In preaching, even as we take creative license, we ultimately offer words based upon various information we've gleaned from and about a text. In preaching we do not rely on simply "what I think about this passage." Instead, we blend our encounter with a passage, with a tradition's narration of it. Tradition is used here in multiple senses, including the community's tradition, scholarly tradition, and personal histories of interpretation. The ability to track down the interpretation of a text is a key element in sermon preparation. Tracking down a text is a means of performing a "check and balance" of the overall message's validity. It also helps preachers demonstrate knowledge of the received tradition and potentially counter opposition to messages that are "against the grain" of the immediate tradition. For instance, if I am going to preach against a text, I must also acknowledge or be aware of how the text has been readily interpreted within the community. At the same time, knowledge of the inherited tradition of scripture provides limitations to the extent of the preacher's play on and interpretation of scripture, even as it simultaneously opens up possibilities of interpretation. The preacher may already have a framework for interpreting a text, whether she recognizes it or not. And that framework may box in her inclinations of interpretation.

There are two crucial contributions to preaching from "tracking down the text." First, in tracking down a text, the preacher begins placing her individual interpretation in conversation with other interpretations, moving toward discerning validity in interpretation through community. After all, the Bible is our story and my story, and it only truly remains as such if the ongoing life of the entire community is attended to in preaching. The need for both the recognition and the ongoing engagement between differing interpretations is evidenced in history. As social location cannot be stripped from biblical interpretations, all interpretations are "autobiographical," whether or not their autobiographical nature is acknowledged.[24]

European middle- and upper-class men have often hidden the *autobiographical* nature of interpretation through purporting the *objective* nature of interpretation. These interpretations do not account for the experiences and reading of the Bible by those on the margins, thus limiting their import and authority in the lives of those on the margins, while they more often inflict harm than create good news.[25] These power dynamics exist within the larger activity of engaging scripture in general and within subcultures of those "on the margins," as we ignore our biases in interpretation.[26] De La Torre offers that correction comes in putting normative interpretations in conversation with the interpretations of those "on the margins," liberating both the underprivileged and privileged. For example, the interpretation of a text by a black heterosexual cisgender man within a male-centered black church tradition may be different from the interpretation of a black lesbian cisgender woman in that same tradition. Ultimately, interpretation is influenced by experience, which, unavoidably, must be acknowledged as we engage scripture; but we are only able to truly explore the limits and possibilities of interpretation as we are in community and conversation with others.

Second, as the imagination is continually engaged in the preaching process, the preacher increases her ability to make imaginative connections about the import and possibilities of scripture's meaning within her community as she explores additional resources. These thoughts of possibility and import evolve as we test our claims, hunches, and inclinations through information gathering and conversations. LaRue states that "informed reflection unleashes imaginative potential" as it places before the preacher "unlimited ideas and ways of envisioning" a text.[27] This is the time when the preacher "brings the formal tools of study" to the interaction with scripture, including people, dictionaries, commentaries, lexicons, and articles.[28] In this phase of study, as the preacher sifts through information, she is able to determine new insights, including what is pertinent and impertinent, what has possibilities, and what poses limitations.

Considering the autobiographical nature of interpretation and the power and privilege inherent in the ability to write and publish, a preacher needs to give attention to variety in both resource materials and the resources that may not be "in print" but are a part of the community's interpretive history. Attending to print resources and "nonprint" communal resources assists the preacher in attending to the tradition of scripture in its normative and marginal traditions of interpretation. At this juncture, the preacher is continuing the work as an ethnographer while reading the signs and symbols of the community and tradition.[29]

IN PRACTICE
Tracking Down the Text

Here are practical steps for tracking down a text:

1. Write down anything you already know about the social location, setting, time, or characters within the passage.

2. Write down anything you know about how and where the passage is usually referenced within the community or faith tradition. Also consider the significant times when members of the community reference the passage (i.e., in passing phrases; in abbreviated forms; during funerals, weddings, and pastoral situations when preached or referenced).

3. Based on what has been determined thus far in tracking down the text, what do you need to learn more about? Is there anything you *want* to learn more about? Consult actual people, commentaries, dictionaries, and articles written by individuals from various gendered, ethnic, and cultural social locations.

4. Be sure to continue the imaginative process as you explore resources, make connections, and explore the meaning of your engagement with scripture.

At the end of this process, the hope is that we allow scripture and the daily life world to be mutually influential in the process of interpretation. The process of engaging scripture functions as our point of reference because we are making decisions about the main message we wish to preach and the best ways to illuminate that message. The process of interpreting scripture can be maximized within a group setting in which multiple people are able to dialogue around a particular passage. The more opportunities we have to make play on and with scripture, the greater our level of comfort will be in engaging the Bible as our story and its lively possibilities in our midst.

Creative Intelligence and Interpretation

Preachers often utilize familiar experience—or that which people know through life and living—to amplify or unearth meaning from their engagement with a passage of scripture. The use of that which is familiar makes the text and larger sermon theme accessible to listeners. The task of the preacher is, first, to claim the meanings of texts as something we have the ability to access in sermon development; and second, to make the text accessible to listeners via preaching. The preacher must determine how to use familiar experience in relation to interpreting scripture. Such choices are especially significant when a preacher's own knowing requires subverting interpretations that lend to their own death or inability to participate fully in the community of faith and world writ large.

The one who preaches as perceived outsider uses typical strategies of interpreting texts alongside life, while having to strategically use what they know about life, the text, and community for promoting a more expansive framework of interpreting scripture. We engage in this type of translational process through preaching by narrating life at various levels of proximity to scripture, and through various modalities. The use of lived experiences not only facilitates the process of unearthing meaning *with* a text but also helps broaden an understanding of whose lives are significant when attending to scripture.

When interpreting texts, the preacher needs the capacity to move among worlds of language, symbols, and images for the sake of communication and translating ideas. Code switching is known within some black communities as the capacity to move between grammar codes and syntax privileged within white frameworks and those privileged within frameworks of black vernacular and dialects. At its core, code switching requires the imaginative intelligence to know when and how to speak two languages and how to transport ideas between language worlds and systems. In a similar manner, Mae Henderson describes black women's ability to communicate in spite of difference as "speaking in tongues." She recovers the biblical idea as a way of describing the "simultaneity of discourse" in the writing of black women when engaging spheres of racial and gendered difference.[30] This same simultaneity of action and movement exists in the preaching of black women.

In interpreting scripture, the work of the preacher is that of using creative intelligence in imagining a multivalent conversation between scripture and the world of the listeners. And it is a conversation with one aim in mind. That aim is to limit the obstacles to scripture being a living document with ongoing salvific effects here and now.

chapter 5
Finding "A Word from the Lord" for Today

We often speak of a sermon's main message, focus, claim, or idea. And the penultimate message in preaching is often referred to as *good news*. Good news is not always good in terms of the feeling it produces; sometimes it is good because the community has discerned it as being qualitatively connected to the gospel. For instance, the assertion that God both grieves and identifies with creation does not necessarily produce joyful, warm, or welcoming feelings; however, the assertion does interject itself into our experiences of life and both reorients and reinterprets those experiences in view of God and faith. The manner in which the good news is communicated and how we fill in its content are the ways by which we shape and reshape that which a community considers meaningful; yes, this shaping involves crafting the overall meaning or good news for an individual sermon, but it also involves shaping that which is overall significant to a community beyond any given sermon. The best practices of preaching have a trajectory and shape good news for the long view.

Giving earnest consideration to the way in which the experiences of black women intersect with the work of interpreting scripture and mining the everyday world for the purposes of preaching assumes a certain ethic inherent to preaching. Namely, we are left with the criteria that preaching does not exist for the sake of itself, but somehow preaching is accountable to life on the ground because life itself is sacred. Therefore, the utterances

chapter 5

it brings forth must ring clear and true for today. Preaching hopes to offer good news for here and now, while assuming that the sermon has some import for the everyday lives of listeners.

There is an understood expectation established between preacher and listener. A word from the Lord is needed or desired. And the preacher is the one sent forth to help amplify such a word. When the preacher returns with the sermon their work is not simply to deliver a message. Part of their work is to deliver a message that shows forth immanence, or relevance and accessibility, in the life of the community. The manner by which a message demonstrates such immediacy or closeness is by way of its texture. This texture includes language, how sentences flow and connect, and the overall arc of the message. The preacher has to determine both the significant message for today and the means of conveying such a message. In short, there is some form of truth a preacher hopes to offer and listeners expect to encounter. Just as life has a pulse, sermons that attend to life have their own pulse, and it is this pulse to which both preacher and listeners attune themselves.

In preaching we make creative use of a community's understanding of the nature of preaching and how that community deems one worthy of preaching. The preacher scaffolds the message in such a way that it works with listener expectations while pushing through the hesitation to imagine the message as true and right fitting. In this regard it almost cannot be denied as "a word from the Lord" for today. The approach is one of intent and purpose.

Coercion is not the basis of an undeniable message that pushes through resistance. Instead, the preacher is attentive to carving out places for the message to land with poignancy, as the message itself takes on the movement and texture of bearing witness in the presence of listeners and their lives. And it bears witness based on what listeners already believe and know to be true, even if the final resting place of a message expands a community's understanding of good news. The content, right-fittingness, and texture of a message are inextricably linked. The very texturing of a message enables listeners and preacher to rise to meet each other in an exchange of affirmation in the preaching moment.

"Something is at stake" is the inherent assumption that informs the intent, content, and pulse of this approach to preaching. Life is at stake, whether it is the life of the preacher, the life of her listener, or the lives of those her listeners will encounter. Preaching that attends to life hanging in the balance does not "come through the back door" in terms of leaving ample room for open-ended possibilities and conclusions about what is at stake or significant. This preaching makes the gospel plain for here and now and moves that message into plain view for listeners, while listeners ultimately affirm or deny the vitality of the message. The preacher moves straight through the front door with her convictions in order to deliver affirming, alternative, expanded, or new frameworks of the good news as the community understands it. A sermon is preached because there is a place where or out of which it speaks in the life of the community.

This place may be life at the pain and grief of its deepest fissures, life at the joy and delight of its highest mountain peaks, or simply the life of faith as it moves about in the mundane. The sermon lands in the lives of individuals and gains traction in those very spaces. With this in mind, the message enacts itself upon the preacher first. For the preacher's life in both its fissures and peeks are part and parcel to the litmus test of good news. The preacher is the first line of checks and balances. This means the preacher has to determine if the message has a sense of trustworthy and right-fitting veracity in their own life.

The preacher must feel a type of immediacy in the presence of the message they seek to deliver before they can communicate such a message and its immediacy. For those who preach from the most fringed spaces within a community there is an acute intersection among that which is at stake, the life of the preacher, and the life of the community. This reality is one of the most significant for black women who preach; for if a message cannot be right fitting for the spectrum of black women in the community, then it cannot be right fitting or true for the community. It cannot be right fitting for the community because it is not recognized as such by the entire community. In a community oriented around God's desire for life over death, if black women must reject a message based on the premise of life over death, the entire community must reject it on the very same premise. Likewise, the community affirms together the immediate possibilities of life in the presence of good news.

And yet, a message risks rejection as it possesses the potential to push or expand harmful borders and assumptions that have allowed some to be included at the expense of others. Therefore, the preacher works to discover what can hold as true and significant in conversation with the Gospel, as they also work to make a path for that truth to be received. This "not yet path" is often straight through a community's unimaginative resistance while making the way straight to the expansion of its most foundational beliefs. The sermon is both accountable to the community and yet unyielding in its aim. Life abundant is both the hope of preaching and that to which the sermon is accountable.

The pulse of preaching for the sake of life is *communally assertive*. Its foundation is in a shared understanding of responsibility between the one who proclaims and the listening community. It takes seriously the responsibility not only to "make it plain" but also to make it plain with and for the community at hand. Its means of communication is confident without naiveté, present and direct, while creating opportunity for the sermon itself to make way for the good news laid bare. This creative edge of preaching offers a nuance to long deployed descriptions that categorize sermons and preaching styles as either authoritarian or communal.

Very Present Truth

The preacher's ability to attend to the pulse of a message is just as significant as her ability to interpret scripture and the world around them. The movement and texture of the message itself seeks to convey its "here and now" relevancy. Sermons within these categories possess immediacy in terms of how and where they touch the ground, as well as a sense of urgency that prompts the community's buy-in as it relates to the relevance, worthiness, and significance of a message in their lives. Sermon import, content, and language make up the texture of a message. The message texture is namely how the message encounters the full bodily knowing of listeners and how language facilitates that encounter in part.

Finding "A Word from the Lord" for Today

Our choices about language, its use, and execution require serious consideration when communicating a very present message. In explaining methods of teaching and learning preaching in traditions of black apprenticeship, Dale P. Andrews asserts such traditions exist "around the encounter of constructive communication and experiential listening."[1] In short, preaching is a phenomenological moment that assumes encountering proclamation is predicated on participation with the experiences of a community. The use of language attempts to bring expression to those familiar experiences in the preaching moment for the sake of an encounter with God's revelation.[2] Language never fully satisfies our hopes even as it is a significant factor.

Language, symbols, ideas, and imagery only get us approximately close to the thing we ultimately hope to say and communicate. Language is elusive. It never quite captures the fullness of a thought. Yet language is the medium we use to signal toward an idea and experience the best that we are able. For instance, the word *God* does not fully capture what we intonate toward regarding a free moving spirit and force that creates and regenerates, attends to creation, and is present in our midst. But we use the insufficiency of one capital letter and three lower case letters to point toward that which we seek to describe as an entirely other, holy, and sacred force. And one has an experience when they encounter the compilation *G-o-d*. One also has an experience based on the way in which *G-o-d* is encountered. For instance, what came before it? What emotions accompanied it? Did it land with a hard thud? or soft vibration? While language is always insufficient, we do have to consider how to remove unnecessary obstacles and what is most required to get us closest to that which we hope is received at the end of a sermon.

In some ways the texture of the sermon helps move listeners into the presence of a message or helps move a message into the presence of listeners. Sermons are an encounter with more than an idea being communicated; in the best practices a sermon connects to all our ways of knowing—including body, mind, spirit, and heart. If sacred-in-breaking brings freedom and alternative futures, the message must ring as one that helps freedom and alternative futures break-in. That which helps makes this ringing true possible has a qualitative nature, just as the good news itself. The nature of proclamation is inherently that which is recognized or revealed as such when we are in its presence. Therefore, the sermon, a medium of proclamation, is rendered in such a way that it facilitates almost a tangible quality to the message—a very present and experiential truth.

(Re)Imaginings for Here and Now

Similar to engaging scripture, tethering preaching to its accountability to the lived experience of the community offers preachers some freedom in their ministerial authority. They demonstrate that accountability through the sermon itself. This means that the message is rarely shrouded in passive or temporary proposals. And yet, this does not negate a malleable understanding of the way in which the beliefs of a community are shaped and reshaped over time.

The authority by which preachers render this form of confident message is grounded in an implicit understanding between the preacher and listener about the preaching task. A narrative of preacher-listener understanding runs something like: the preaching task primarily involves "we the gathered community" trusting that "you the preacher" have spent time in study and prayer and now have "a word from the Lord." Within this overarching narrative, the sermon responds to expectations regarding the preaching moment as the message is offered in a forthright way, as opposed to assuming power not given to the preacher.

The pulse of a sermon that attends to what is at stake in life possesses a distinctive feel and movement. The language is active not passive. The language is direct and present. The sermons show forth a reality as opposed to talking about an idea from a distance. The message possesses a "right-nowness" as it attends to that which hangs in the balance.

Direct and Present Language

When we are in the presence of speech that possesses a type of immediacy, there is a qualitative nature to its characteristics. The language is often firm or resolute; the movement and direction of the argument may seem clear without much nuance around the direction the message is moving. Direct and present language in preaching has an implication for not only the pulse of the message but also the relationship between the biblical world and today's world. Here engaging scripture and using lived experience meet anew for the sake of making good news plain. Neither the text nor today's world can supersede the other as they relate to naming truth as it emerges at the intersection of the two and to making meaningful proclamation. Instead, somewhere in the wrestling between the two worlds, whatever emerges has immediate implications on and for the lives of their listeners. These implications take shape in a direct or impending claim about the gospel message. The truth preaching communicates is good news or gospel in the here and now.

Working within this trajectory, Vicki's sermon "Oil for Pouring" contains confident speech and takes on a level of immediacy. Not only is the message designed for those gathered, but also it has immediate implications for their lives. Vicki preaches from the passage of scripture found in Mark 14:3-9, in which a nameless woman anoints Jesus with costly ointment and receives criticism from onlookers. As Vicki ends her sermon, she states her penultimate message:

> I'm so glad about it because God is not a respecter of person. What Jesus did for her, God will do for you. Today is your day. Today, if you hear my voice, harden not your hearts, Today is your day—it's your day to forgive past hurts, and to produce some oil.
>
> It's your day to move beyond guilt and shame and to produce some oil. It's your day to come out of destructive relationships and produce some oil. —Vicki

The message is that God will do for those gathered what Jesus did for the woman who anointed him with oil. God will offer forgiveness and remove guilt so that believers may have an offering of expensive oil in the form of a testimony. She affirms that "today is" the day for those who are gathered to offer forgiveness and be forgiven by God. Today is their day to move beyond guilt and destructive relationships. Her message is not one

chapter 5

for future action, nor does it hold the possibility of something occurring later. In fact, it is quite the opposite. The preacher makes her claim as a factual statement for that very moment of delivery, using present-tense language. Her claim is based on scripture and her understanding of this message possessing immediate implications for the lives of those gathered. In this scenario, the preacher's claim collapses the time among scripture, the ongoing activity of God, and the listeners' world. The good news of God's activity in the lives of believers is accessible and relevant right then, right there, and on that very day.

As Vicki declares an immediate accessibility to present divine activity, Barbara formulates her message as a command to immediate action for those gathered who find themselves "Against All Odds." She begins with the question, "What should you do when you're against all odds?" and follows with an expository exploration of 2 Chronicles 20, which recounts the story of King Jehoshaphat and Israel going into battle. Barbara introduces the question, then gives her listeners a direct message of instruction. Her message of instruction is based on her interpretation of the biblical story and what King Jehoshaphat would tell those gathered. With clarity and forthrightness she states:

What do you do?

Stand up! . . . I encourage you today to stand up like Jehoshaphat. . . . [Y]ou may be standing with shaky knees but just stand up and declare the goodness of the Lord and watch God move on your behalf.

. . . Stand still! . . . He (God) says, "you don't have to fight this battle. We have to just stand still in the area of righteousness. . . .

. . . After you stand up against the enemy and stand still in battle, it's time to start singing! Verse 22, "as they began to sing and praise, the Lord set ambushes against the men of Ammon and Moab." —Barbara

Barbara uses imperative, assertive, and deductive forms of language and delivery as a means to instruct, if not command, those gathered to "Stand up!" "Stand still!" and "Start Singing!" in their current adverse situations. "You!" is the implied person and the direct answer to the question of "who is to stand up, stand still, and start singing." "Now" is the implied time and direct answer to the question of "when to stand up, stand still, and start singing." The good news the preacher communicates is not something to ponder or something that has future implications. The good news has a direct recipient and calls for immediate action.

For our preachers, the gospel breaks into their lives and the lives of their listeners. Their claims about good news have immediate implications for very present life circumstances. Direct, assertive, and active speech is congruent with understandings of immediate implications, and this is the means through which the women deliver good news. Passive and less forthright methods may not have the same force in emphasizing the immediacy of good news and its literal impact on today, during this very hour, and in this very moment.

Of course in the worse practices of preaching anything can be used in a way that is destructive to the thriving of the community or used as a method of inculcation instead of helping generative possibilities break forth in the community. Such things happen in communities of faith. The search for language that is direct, present, and immediate in quality does not inherently mean abusive, over and against, or disregard of self and other. Preaching for the sake of sustaining life cannot have these realities as their end. Preaching that attends to the immediacy of life is accountable to the lives it engages and the spirit it dares to conjure.

Confidence without Naiveté

For those who preach as "the outsider," their use of language must possess the texture of immediacy for the listeners at hand, as their messages are constantly assessed for validity. The anticipation of a word from the Lord and the preacher's attention to texturing the message make its reception possible. Yet such immediacy intonates toward the nature of the message being a God-message offered by a finite messenger who has a responsibility to the community to whom she preaches. The pulse of the sermon is carried forward with a type of confidence without naiveté. The uncertain hope of both listener and preacher is in God's message arriving

chapter 5

to the places in which we lay most in wait for a word from the Lord. For our preachers here, we will find that this hope may be communicated as directly as "God's message is . . .," "God says . . .," or by the more subtle, but no less direct, way the precision of the message is communicated. This precision manifests in terms of both how the message intersects with the lives of listeners and how the preacher carves out this intersection.

Louise makes use of this combination in a very explicit manner in her sermon "Postponement and Reconciliation," in which, she ultimately claims: "Delay is not denial." The opening words of the sermon establish Louise's authority as a preacher and the authority of her message:

> My sisters and my brothers, I have come to you this morning with a word from the Lord. —Louise

Louise is the one who brings a message to those gathered that morning. The message is not any message, but "a word from the Lord." This "word from the Lord" indicates the significance of the preacher's message and its sacredness. Louise is not about to make ordinary speech and claims; instead she gives her listeners something she believes to be sacred and holy. And with her opening disclaimer she calls the attention of those gathered to the significance of the message she is about to deliver. Simply reading her message as a deductive and authoritarian message misses the implied nuance between the listener's hope and the preacher's message.

For Louise, her listeners have been waiting and have experienced delay in their lives as it relates to the promises of God coming to fruition. Although she does not promise her listeners that this day is the day of the fulfillment of those promises, she does relay to them that there is a word for today: "I would declare to each of us *today that delay is not denial*," she tells them. Her words are in many regards an immediate offering of accessible hope. While the individuals wait on God, who does not move on their timetable, they need to know that, in this moment, delay is not denial because God is presently waiting and monitoring their situations, which Louise expresses in her statement, "God *has* you on the radar screen."

Louise opens with and maintains very confident speech in both the message she is delivering and in her assignment, even as she communicates an understanding that she interprets and makes best guesses about the scripture and the definitive message.

She retains the use of *I* even as she maintains that the message is a divine one:

> We are continuing our journey with Jesus to Jerusalem and I contend that all of the things that occurred on the journey are part of the Divine plan of God for his son Jesus. In the midst of my preparation for the text that is before us this morning, *I* believe that *I* see through the actions of Jesus postponement and reconciliation.
>
> My friends, do you believe that God has a plan for your life? Then *I* would declare to each of us today that delay is not denial. *I* believe that God is expecting our actions to align with the word of the Lord, but He also wants it to be our will. *I* believe that God's Plan is being done for us through the Reconciliation of the many issues that plague our lives. —Louise

Louise communicates that the message is her belief and contention about what is truth, as she marks herself as the one declaring, believing, and contending the message. As a messenger on assignment, the preacher is offering "a word" to the gathered community—those she refers to as "friends" and "my sisters and my brothers." Although Louise does not fully evoke an egalitarian or collaborative understanding of herself as one interpreter amongst many interpreters, her more assertive communication style does not inherently retain ignorance of her being one individual within a larger community to which her interpretation is responsible.

As one understands that preaching and proclamation are only possible by way of God, she is always aware of the message delivered by way of the messenger. Instances of confident speech are not necessarily indicative of the preacher's arrogance and, on the contrary, could often demonstrate understanding the real importance of the task and message being communicated. Our preachers seem to have an understanding that there is weightiness in the preaching moment and little room to communicate an "untruth." Vicki literally shares both the struggle of her preparation and insight as to how and where she has derived the confidence that the message at hand in her sermon "Oil for Pouring," is truly a message from God:

> I wrestled with God and I asked politely for another message. I asked for another text, I begged God for relief and I rhetorically questioned whether or not God really intended for me to preach this particular message. I was in the vice grip for weeks when God finally spoke in the cool of the evening and reminded me that this message is not about me, not as much as it is about you. It is not a message to tantalize you but one to teach you. It's not designed to cause you to languish but to launch you into liberation. The message today, "Oil for the Pouring," is taken from the Mark's Gospel and has been prepared precisely with you in the mind of God. —Vicki

She depicts herself as "wrestling with God," asking for another message and begging for relief. In preparation for the sermon, she describes herself as being in search of the intentions of God in preaching "this particular message." The preacher affirms that not only did God confirm the message, but also God "spoke" to her in "the cool of the evening," reminding her of the greater purposes of the preaching task. This preaching moment and message were given specifically for those gathered as they were "in the mind of God," which supersedes her will as a preacher. She is accountable to both God and the people of God. With the explication of her struggle, Vicki reveals the source of her confidence in the message she is speaking—namely, her time with God. From struggling with God, she is confident even in uncertainty that this message is for those to whom she speaks.

In one respect, Vicki is merely communicating what most of her listeners would assume and would hope took place during her time of preparation. Listeners trust the preacher has prayed, studied, and spent time with God; indeed, it is the trust of listeners that grants the preachers the ability to have liberty with confident speech. There is an assumption present between the preacher and her listeners that the message being communicated is a message from God, and the preacher has received her word from the Lord. And for this preacher in particular, the message is one that affirms both the people of God in the mind of God and teaching for the sake of their liberation.

While preaching for the sake of life is shrouded in and carried forward by speech that has an impulse of confidence as it involves direct language and immediate implication, the preacher remains accountable to conditions and agreement made between she and listeners about her tasks and responsibility to the community in preaching. In this framework listeners may have little to no room for the assumption that this is not the message for which the preacher was responsible for delivering. Yet the preacher is ultimately responsible to the task entrusted to her by the community. The speech is neither naive nor authoritarian, resisting the fallacy of assuming the legitimacy of all preached ideas.

Building up to Good News

Confident and direct language does not negate nuance and buildup, nor does it necessarily demand deductive logic. If truth and the word must be the word for all in the community, the preacher may need to work at bringing "all on board" and along the way, especially when there has been resistance and exclusion in the community. Therefore, the preacher has to attend to building up to the good news by layering one's claim in small increments at a time. For instance, if a preacher wants to push the envelope on the issue of same-sex marriage in her community, she must first determine that which the community most believes and can affirm about humanity and relationships. And from there she must gain affirmation of the good news until she makes it to the ultimate claim about same-sex marriage. In preaching we might attend to the pulse of the message through description or by storytelling that elongates an idea or by using shorter sentences with crisp language and imagery that make a thought concise and tangible. This buildup makes use of the world of the text and the world of listeners.

As previously explored, there are times when a preacher needs to preach against a text. To do this effectively she has to determine how to bring listeners along. This often involves having to build up to good news in spite of the text or resistance from listeners to the ultimate claim. If we revisit Vicky's sermon "The Silence We Keep," there is an opportunity to place her choices in conversation with the use of direct and confident language that relies upon buildup to help listeners arrive with the preacher at a right-fitting message for here and now. Vicky uses buildup to declare that good news cannot be found in a particular passage of scripture. However, she uses buildup in the same manner as it would be expected in the tradition, as it relates to elongating the narrative that leads up to her major claims. Vicki combines the use of building up to her gospel claim with an understanding that the gospel of the here and now may require us to reject the circumstances portrayed in scripture. She uses the story of Tamar's rape in 2 Samuel 13:19-20 to claim the good news at present day.

As far as timing, Vicki devotes half of her sermon to building up to the claim, that, namely: Because we understand the tragedy of sexual violence and silence, we must make decisions different than those recounted in Tamar's story. Vicki declares that the good news is that "Tamar lived in a different time than we do now," with "a situation of life far different than ours." And, because of this, "Our response to sexual violence within our family does not have to be the same as hers." However, in order to reject the condition of scripture being a model template, Vicki takes great care to recount the story and times of Tamar and the present-day actions of her listeners prior to saying that the scripture passage is not good news here and now. In order for her to successfully preach against the passage, she lures her listeners into the disgust and tragedy of Tamar's situation. Essentially, she *paints the picture* for those listening through adjectives and words that engage the senses of seeing, hearing, and touching. Tamar did not "take to bed" or "lay with Amnon"; nor was she just "raped." Vicki recounts Tamar's being "forcibly raped by her brother" and "violated" in "a place one presumes offers safety and protection for womankind." Vicki then describes a "bedraggled, surely bruised and humiliated" Tamar, with a "torn" once "beautiful garment that only the King's daughters were allowed to wear," who now goes about "wailing loudly" only to find "a salve and the balm" of "frustration and agony" in keeping silent.

At this moment, surely, Vicki's listeners can see, feel, and agree that Tamar's situation is one of tragedy. It is here that Vicki turns to those gathered to say that, at present, they too have allowed victims to suffer in silence and be unsafe in their own households in order to protect the larger reputation of the community. Because of this silent suffering, communities will continue to lose the "great thinkers, dreamers, preachers, artists, daughters, and sons." Since listeners can agree to the tragedy of Tamar's story and now see the tragedy of Tamar's story being repeated in their own communities, it is without question that the story of scripture cannot be good news today; instead, good news must be brought to the passage. Vicki achieves this by explaining how those silenced by abuse can gain voice, since the good news is that we no longer need to be silent.

Vicki's use of buildup is savvy: she uses the tools and methods of a narrative preaching tradition to offer an interpretation of scripture that is not normative when compared to the interpretation and proclamation of good news made by other preachers. Vicki's choices provide insight into how preachers not only use the tools and structures of a tradition to convey a message but also use the same tools and structures to critique or alter a tradition of thought and practice. Yes, good news that has immediate implications is important, but Vicki changes the source of that good news; the source is no longer scripture, but the wisdom from her and her listener's familiar experiences.

Although black preaching is understood to rely on more assertive forms of delivery, both slow delivery and buildup are aspects of this assertive style, and both elongate the message. When discussing slow delivery, Mitchell describes this as the literal rate of delivery, as in speed.[3] The preacher uses intentional delay in pacing and moves toward more climactic moments, crystallizing the sermon's idea(s) of truth. The penultimate climactic moment in this framework is the point of celebration, which I discussed in chapter 3 as the use of familiar experience. Storytelling and using detail are identifiable tools that influence the rate and pace at which truth claims are reached and contribute to the effect of buildup. Building up and filling in the story, as described above and in chapter 4, are characteristics of these more assertive preaching traditions and meter the forthrightness of the preacher's direct speech.

Confident utterances, immediacy, and buildup are interworking parts in the pulse of preaching. However, in preaching, we remain aware of self-imprint in the process of preaching, in terms of truth being channeled through a messenger and offered to the community for its engagement. This awareness includes understanding ourselves as finite beings with emotions, biases, and proclivities wrestling for a message of integrity. Yet the preacher is called to embrace human limitations and confidence within those limitations. We dare to offer an utterance because of what remains at stake if the message is not preached and the community's trust launches one into the deep to discern a word. The hope is for both the preacher and community to arrive together at a word that has integrity before God.

Ingenuity and Truth Telling

Preaching that assumes contemporary veracity—or the presence of truth that resonates with the here and now realities—disrupts former dichotomies drawn between authoritarian and communal descriptions of message development and authority. Indeed, this form of preaching has a particular presence and impact; yet it is not disconnected from a responsibility to the community to determine the parameters or boundaries of how preaching takes shape in its midst; its pulse is both communal and assertive. In the best practices of communally-assertive forms of preaching the preacher is able to help move the community from a listening disposition of "over and against," or speaker and passive receiver, to a collaborative model of truth finding and declaring. This shift is most possible when the rhetorical style of preaching is joined with actual content of preaching that espouses mutual and collaborative premises of faith and human relationships, in terms of affirming the presence of everyone at the table in a framework of equity and justice.

Historically, some would describe the ministerial authority in black preaching traditions as assertive. If women who preach in such assertive black preaching traditions opt not to use this form of truth conveyance, they risk not speaking in the language of their communities. Here "speaking the language" is not necessarily about pitch, tone, voice, volume, and the like, but more so about the way in which the language is structured and how this structure shapes the sermon's movement and pulse as well as listener process. Speaking in an outsider language would influence their perceived credibility based on insider belonging. If the preacher loses credibility with her listeners, authority is undercut and there is a risk of creating unreceptive listeners.

Because women's bodies and speech are still contested within pulpit spaces, the women's use of more traditional assertive approaches to truth, based in their communities' traditions, becomes the vehicle through which their voices and claims are heard and possibly received. To an extent, the tradition shapes understandings of truth and how it is conveyed, and the preacher uses that same understanding with her own pitch to articulate what she claims is the most urgent matters to the community. In this, the preacher retools what she has inherited for her pulpit purposes of communicating the gospel.

It has been argued that within the framework of black preaching traditions the preacher is granted a license by listeners to *make it plain* in telling the gospel, which entails a generous amount of liberty in the "thought provoking exchange of ideas between the text, the congregation, and the preacher."[4] The intent is to help listeners "understand and identify" the good news.[5] There is a sense in which the preacher is an expert and is granted the ability to speak from a more assertive and propositional position.[6]

On the other hand, some preaching literature and listening styles favor a more lateral and conversational approach to conveying truth.[7] Within this framework, truth is malleable and grounded within the authority of the community's interrogation, even truth offered by the preacher. Truth emerges and is created through the means of mutual community engagement. In the most literal practices of these collaborative models preaching is dialogical and conversational. Here, the preacher is an individual and interpreter, while the community, as a group of individuals and valid interpreters, is held in close relationship to the preacher. In explicit conversational approaches the assumption is that truth emerges from the work of both the preacher and listener together.

In light of these assumptions about authority in preaching, it seems easy to draw divides between hierarchical and communal styles of preaching. Instead of creating dichotomies, communal-assertive frameworks of preaching make the gospel plain and do so in such a way that it opens itself up to being constantly interrogated by and answerable to those who are the least thriving members of a community. The use of language for preaching is not communal or assertive; instead it is both communal *and* assertive, as it brings listeners along on the discovery of good news.

When black women preach within frameworks of life and death or thriving and demise, there is a way in which they must attend to the urgency of such manners within the confines of traditions that recognize these frameworks. The expectations within the communities to which they are trusted to bring a divine message grant preachers license to use direct and confident speech, which could be perceived as intrusive or assuming by outsiders. The choice to portray truth claims in a more direct and assertive manner is logical if this is the primary means by which communities delineate, interrogate, and receive speech presented as truth. However, most important, immediacy in language leads the way if something genuinely hangs in the balance.

(Re)Imagining Sermon Development

Listeners expect to hear some significant message, which they both recognize and deem as the sermon's takeaway or inspiration. This will ultimately be called "true" or "truth" or, on its best days, *proclamation*. At any given moment, when conveying an idea, a preacher is acknowledging the existence of truth in a community, promoting a certain kind of truth, and responding to a truth already present within a community (to affirm, expand, or refute it).[8] This truth entails a delineation of the meaning of the gospel—which is sometimes in part and, at other times, whole—through language and symbols.

The means of conveying truth and the places in which truth is revealed arrange the content, timing, and movement of the sermon, which characterize the pulse of a message. For instance, one preacher may only divulge a "glimmer" of the real message during a segment of the sermon, then slowly reveal the rest of the claim, while another preacher may show all of his or her cards up front and then explain the claims just revealed. Therefore, not only is the content of a truth claim significant in terms of what the preacher deems as the meaning of the gospel, but also how this meaning is revealed by metering the sermon's style and ultimately the preacher's use of authority is just as important. A preacher helps the community make sense of, and make meaning from, life in relationship to faith as she attends to the literal content of the message, its development, and experience it invokes. Those who preach as outsiders do not have the luxury of insignificant or less precise messages, nor should the best practices of preaching offer such messages.

Listening is a cultural act. We learn to listen based on how we have been conditioned to listen by our communities. Therefore, a preacher is in conversation with a community's general understanding of sermon form, pacing, intonation, and shape even as they are determining the form, pacing, content, and shape of any given sermon. In preaching we push to render the immediacy of a message recognizable by a community; yet we push for such recognition while being aware of the nature of preaching as a task reliant on God. Nevertheless, we are held accountable to the hope of preaching by the community. In this, preaching authority is tied to communal relationships while it asserts the necessity and relevance of an utterance from God for today. Even as we have been taught to listen in particular ways and have expectations of the general pulse of a sermon (i.e., inductive, deductive, narrative form, or three delineated points), every sermon has the opportunity to make the good news plain and evident to listeners in an immediate manner. The work of the preacher is to determine what choices make the message most accessible and tangible right here and right now in this place and at this time.

This approach to determining the sermon's message and then texturing that message requires the preacher to locate the significance of the message. An inherent assumption exists at the forefront of sermon development, and that assumption is, "Truth must be recognized as truth on this day." A message possesses authority and opens new possibilities within a community, in so far as it is immediately relevant.

First, the immediacy within this way of constructing and developing a message assumes there is something at stake in hearing or not hearing the message; therefore, the preacher must determine *what's at stake*. Second, when something *is* at stake, the message brings with it the possibility of influence, new direction, and new vision, and the preacher engages in a type of *possibility thinking* in search of these options. Third, the possibilities that the message brings are not general or abstract, but possibility itself is woven into very particular areas of the life of the community; the message takes root in specific places even as it has the opportunity to expand and evolve in unforeseen places. In the preparation stage the preacher determines potential places for the message *taking root and growing roots*. Finally, after determining the very particular areas of the community's life to which the message might speak or ring clear, the next step of texturing the message involves narrating the message through those various points of connection with communal and individual experiences. The preacher attends to what is known about life by *returning to familiar experience*. As a preacher develops their message, what is at stake in the message, the initial visions of possibility that the message creates, where the message will take root, familiar experiences, and attention to these details help support the process of texturing a message with strong connections to present lived experiences. These connections leave room for the listener's imagination to meet the preacher's imagination, expanding the realties the message makes possible in everyday life.

What's at Stake?

Confident speech communicates a level of certainty about a message. And in turn, the implication is that the preacher has taken some ownership of the message and has a sense of conviction about its significance. Using active, present, and indicative speech forms demonstrates a preacher's belief in a message when placed alongside particular themes related to communal life. And in particular when such forms of speech are placed alongside themes related to a community's thriving, on the individual or communal level, the underlying conviction is that something is at stake, which makes the message worthy of being preached. Theme, conviction, and underlying assumptions are the trifecta that shape the pulse of a message, with which listeners are invited to participate.

Preaching for the sake of life assumes an explicit "So what?" even if it is only attended to implicitly in the sermon content. The preacher is clear that there is something hanging in the balance that makes the sermon worth preaching; this knowing then shapes the sermon and its content. In being able to name and locate the significance of their message, a preacher is able to better recognize and own what is at stake in the message for their community.

The "at-stake" aspect of the message includes what makes the message worth listening to and being preached, as well as what hangs in the balance or remains at risk if the message is neither preached nor received. Making plain the significance of a message requires the ability to communicate the authority of a message within the lives of listeners in both concrete and poignant ways that remain responsible to their contexts. A preacher cannot help listeners recognize and locate the significance of her message unless she has first identified the significance of her message in sermon development. Being able to locate what is at stake for the community in a message is the gateway to telling truth that remains purposefully responsible to the community.

The preacher's own experience of the message becomes the initial site of the vision and possibilities opened up by a message. Similarly, in the preacher's experience of the message, one begins to understand the significant possibilities and risks of the message's never manifesting itself in the minds and hearts of the listeners. Because preaching is both an action of God's claim on us and an act of human performance, the preacher as human performer is the first one acted upon. We first make ourselves available to discern and experience the claim on our own lives in sermon preparation and delivery.[9] Where the community hears, receives, and

chapter 5

experiences God's claim is the location of the preacher's investment and conviction in preaching.[10] This very conviction and investment is tied to the risk and possibilities inherent in the message's being preached and not being preached.

Right-here and right-now truth meets and articulates with conviction something about the matters hanging in the balance, as well as something about hope and inspiration. There is a tendency for those on the margins to read the Bible with "what's at stake" in view in very concrete ways for thriving and survival. This hope filled survey of the text is in contrast to surveying the text for general universal truths.[11] Reading for hope attempts to "grasp God in the midst of struggle and oppression."[12] De La Torre states that "when people live under oppressive structures, they turn to the Bible for the strength to survive another day, not to figure out how long a day lasted in Genesis 1."[13] Affirming these same sentiments as a part of the history of African Americans' interpretation of the Bible, Cleophus J. LaRue argues that it is the "daily struggle of survival" that makes the "ring of truth heard" and important within black preaching traditions.[14] The search for hope insinuates that there is something at stake and there is a need for hope to exist.

• •

IN PRACTICE
What's at Stake?

The following are practical helps for determining what's at stake in a message:

1. After narrowing down in a sentence or two the primary message to be preached, ask the following questions:

    What is at stake in this message?

    What hangs in the balance?

2. Because it is entirely possible that something can be "at stake" yet remain relatively insignificant, it is important to ask another set of questions:

Is this message significant?

What difference would it make if the message was never preached or if the message was never received?

Why does it matter?

Why is it important?

3. Because it is important to keep messages experientially focused, it is a good idea to ask another set of questions as well:

Whose lives do you hope the message will affect?

What circumstance(s) might this message affect?

....

Being able to test a message and to attend to core questions about its efficaciousness in an efficient way establishes the foundation of our conviction about the message we bring and reinforces our accountability to locating good news that has authority within the community.

Possibility Thinking

Just as there is something at stake within a message, there is also something to gain and new possibilities to discover if the message is preached and received. As our preachers ushered their listeners to the door of the immediacy of a message, they also open a door that showed forth new possibilities. New possibilities signal that the status quo, present state, or current predicament and are not always ultimately desirable or the final judgment of the way things are, should be, or will be. Through the sermon the preacher seeks to offer a new vision or framework for conceptualizing life and life matters, albeit in sometimes-subtle ways. These new possibilities are the impetus of "good news" or "gospel" within the message and to the community, giving the message a dynamic of inspiration and casting an alternative future. Being able to dream up the possibilities of a message and its claims on the life of the community is of real importance because it moves past the "so what" and helps facilitate memorable and inspiring significance of the message as it relates to God's vision.

The word preached offers something very specific within our lives, specifically a new vision and realm of ordering based on God's hopes and eschatological future.[15] Walter Brueggemann explains the functions of prophets and prophecy in the Hebrew Bible and explores the ways in which the prophetic message was energizing and offered inspiration and hope—even as it sometimes corrected, warped, and distorted cultural narratives. The prophetic message offers a new corrective, or a counter-narrative to the current narrative of the world in which the people of God live. For instance, as the words of Moses critiqued the empire and culture of empire, they simultaneously energized the children of Israel in the vision and trust of the Holy One, even as that vision was not fully known.[16]

One distinction of the prophetic new vision is its particularity: it is written for a community in a very particular place and time.[17] The prophetic is a new vision for the here and now, not for the future by-and-by. It is also a vision of possibility and imagination;[18] this is the nature of the prophetic imagination. The prophetic imagination ushers in the gospel or good news; at its core it is theological,[19] as it brings the narrative of God into direct confrontation with the recurring narrative loops within the dominant culture. In one situation, the loop of injustice is confronted with God's desire, preference, and call for justice here and now. In another instance, the loop of hopelessness and despair is confronted by the narrative of relief and hope.

Alyce McKenzie appropriates Charles Bartow's practical theology of proclamation in describing the visionary possibility that motivates and drives preaching and the preaching moment:[20]

> Preaching issues a claim, it directs us toward a future and to Him [*sic*] to whom the future belongs. The referent of a sermon . . . is not something in the past, nor is it any individual thing or circumstance of the present. Instead the referent of a sermon is what lies beyond. Preaching has to do with what yet may be.[21]

In this way, preaching is both performative and evocative; it evokes wonder and possibility as the experience of the community and preacher meet the text and action of God in preaching.

··

IN PRACTICE
Possibility Thinking

In order to explore the visionary possibilities in a sermon's message, you can begin by posing questions to the message that seek to tease out inspiration and vision. Here is a short list:

1. What possibilities are opened up by this message?
2. What promises does this message hold?
3. What makes this message inspiring?
4. What claims does this message make on my life?
5. What new possibilities, visions, or narratives does this message want to create in my experience?"

··

Taking Root, Growing Roots

Preaching for the sake of life seeks out places where the seeds of the message may take root in the lives of individuals, and then attends to those places. The new possibilities that a message brings are concretized through the everyday experiences of individuals. We are able to demonstrate and illuminate the significance of a specific message only as we are able to zoom in on very specific circumstances of human existence; and then, we work within and out of those circumstances as points of contact for the message on the ground. The ability to use life and scripture in tandem with major claims is the vehicle that creates room for truth to be both recognized and experienced, *right here and right now.*

chapter 5

Finding a place for a message to speak and retain pertinence in the community helps listeners identify with the good news, its significance, and its imminence in their lives. The aspects of life, scripture, and gospel claims are difficult to detangle from one another when preaching on the creative edge of a *right here and right now* message. If one is attempting to attend to the connections between the divine pulse of a text and our world, the strands of those connections are fluid. The connections move between the seams of both worlds, as opposed to rigid demarcations that are easily separated out from one another. The result is a message that helps truth lay itself bare within the community.

"Make it plain!" is an audible response from listeners in some black preaching traditions as the preacher calls out her message. The hope of both listener and preacher in these exchanges of call and response is: "Make it plain!"[22] This shout for clarity and poignancy in the preacher's narration of the text, the message, and its immediate import or connection to lived experience. Even in its clarity and poignancy narration leaves room for listener imagination to meet the preacher's imagination, allowing the listener to fill in the relevance of the message for their own life's story. In its best practices "making it plain" affords room for listeners to make their own connections as they are spurred by the preacher's skills of quilting together the pieces of life, text, and claim. Connecting scripture, the message, and lived experience begins with imagining those points of connection.

When a preacher is able to imagine lived experiences in direct relation to the message, they are able to better narrate their message in a way that connects with those lived experiences; envisioning these connections is what affords the preacher the ability to "make it plain." Making it plain helps the message take root or find its root, the place of generative possibility, in the life of the community. In locating where the message may take root, a preacher must simply brainstorm the various life scenarios to which the message may pertain and with which listeners may connect. This brainstorming includes circumstances within the lives of individual people, and circumstances within the life of the community. This brainstorming in practice can be viewed below in conjunction with the practices of returning to familiar experience.

Returning to Familiar Experience: Creating Mutual Experiences

The sermon message is mediated through the preacher's abilities to engage the stories of their listeners alongside the message they hope to convey. The preacher has to attend to the life of both the community and the individual person to effectively narrate and imagine the spaces where good news takes root and opens up possibilities for life today. In the process of narrating and imagining, the preacher elevates individual stories as sacred matters of engagement alongside larger communal narratives; they also move between the personal and communal veracities of good news. The movement between personal and communal is of particular importance when testing the validity of a message for "all" in the community, especially when one intends for a message to be answerable to the possibility of life abundant for all. This movement is primarily undergirded by knowledge and makes use of the individual struggle for daily life and survival and thriving and commonalities in that struggle.

Micro- and macro-level thinking fit into all aspects of sermon development. By this time, the preacher most likely knows the main message they intend to convey and has now begun thinking about the means through which they will convey that message. Therefore, micro- and macro-levels of thinking may be most generative at this juncture as the preacher is better able to fine-tune their use of all four aspects of the sermon in relationship to one another than earlier in the development process.

The movement between the personal and communal in a message provides listeners the opportunity to access the same ideas in alternative forms; this provides another means of both showing and connecting to the immediacy of the good news. Additionally, this personal-communal movement creates a type of mutual experience among and between listeners and the preacher through a community narrative, or sacred story, when one is not readily present or appropriate to engage with contemporary issues. For those preachers who are itinerants, moving from congregation to congregation, being able to create these mutual experiences assists the preacher in making points of connection with listeners when they do not have the opportunity to become deeply immersed within a particular congregation and its sacred stories.

Creating mutual experiences forms a type of common language within the gathered community, which supports listeners' abilities not only to understand the message but also to recognize its veracity through its various points of connection with lived experience. In the process of constructing meaning, a preacher facilitates making a new text visible and available to the community. Availability connotes a text being accessible to listeners. Accessibility is granted through placing familiar experience side by side with a biblical text. This placement is not simply reporting or showing the text but offering meaning (new text) that is forged out of both the biblical text and the contemporary setting.[23] In other words, a preacher permits a text to be seen with *contemporary force and authority*.

There are various means through which a preacher can narrate the relationship among lived experience, scripture, and the message. John McClure refers to this process of making cultural and experiential points of contact with a sermon's meaning as *narrative enculturation*.[24] Narrative enculturation may be considered in two ways, namely, mechanisms and content. First, the actual narrative mechanisms are a means of making "points of contact" between contemporary experience and a sermon's meaning. Narrative mechanisms, including figures of speech and imagery, are used in relationship to that which is familiar to listeners in order to show meaning in sermons.[25] The actual content—stuff—of these narrative mechanisms is the second aspect of narrative enculturation and is of primary concern in creating mutual experience.

How we make points of contact between sermon ideas and lived experiences also includes how we engage both personal and communal aspects of lived experience within narrative mechanisms such as figures of speech, imagery, and storytelling. In creating mutual experience, the choices made about the content of lived experience must attend to both the personal and communal via narrative mechanisms. In part, engaging the personal and communal realities of lived experience in black preaching traditions has facilitated the poignancy and clarity of "making it plain."[26] The effectiveness of creating mutual experiences is in our ability to facilitate points of connection between the message and lived experience with veracity while attending to the multiple aspects of what it means to exists in the world.

The question is: How might a preacher go about the process of exploring the creation of mutual experiences when returning to familiar experience as a means of making room for the right here and now? At this point, the preacher relies on their knowledge of the community, the human condition, and the process of engaging scripture to identify where their message turns up the volume on certain aspects of lived experience. In this way of constructing meaning, the preacher recreates the need or conditions for their message to be received by listeners. Here, learning to tell the human story in a variety of ways is central. This variety could include considering multiple stories that are not explicitly our own in multiple lengths, with varying degrees of specificity and vagueness. For example, if one is speaking of sadness and despair and wants to communicate hope, consider how to depict the instance of sadness and despair in brevity or at length. Then consider ways to narrate a new vision and alternative reality into those same instances of sadness and despair.

This process of truth-telling through exploring experiences encourages the preacher to explore the right-fitting message by considering the ways in which the message has first made a claim on their own life, and then use that knowing as a bridge to the lives of others. In this work, the preacher is convinced of not only the message's significance but also the possibilities the gospel presents for real-life situations hanging in the balance. This conviction then influences one's ability to show the imminence of the message for today. Conveying the message alongside lived experience becomes the means of delivery for a message for *right here and right now*.

chapter 5

IN PRACTICE
Creating Mutual Experience

Creating mutual experiences through preaching is directly related to your engagement with the community and world around you. Pay attention to news stories, engage in people watching, have conversations with others, and simply immerse yourself in community life and spaces. All of these practices help foster the ability to locate spaces within life where a message may speak, take root, and have vibrant possibilities. Here are some practical steps:

1. Jot down specific situations in which this message might have generative possibility, especially places of despair, hope, and discord; matters of provision; or in relationships.

2. List places in the lives of individuals where this message might live and speak.

3. Think about the various groups of individuals who may encounter the message (i.e., children, women, men, LGBTQIA+ persons, singles, partnered, the affluent, and the disenfranchised). Pinpoint specific descriptions of people within a particular group (i.e., a young black transgender girl).

4. Consider how this very specific idea may be engaged from multiple vantage points as it relates to the people or group of people identified.

5. Explore the use of several abbreviated snapshot descriptions, longer descriptions, and a combination of both, and reflect on the way your message conveys truth by creating shared experience.

Immediacy Textured

In preaching we push to render the immediacy of a message recognizable by a community; and we push for such recognition while aware that preaching is a task reliant on God. Nevertheless, we are accountable to the hopes of preaching, and the community holds us accountable in this task. In this, preaching authority is tied to communal relationships while it asserts the necessity and relevance of a word from God for today. The very act of preaching makes use of one being authorized to preach by the community. The preacher relies heavily on the authority a community invests in them for the sake of sermon development and delivery. The ways in which the import of a message and its efficaciousness are communicated are just as significant as the bare-bones content, or claim, of the sermon.

Listeners grant preachers permission to help the significance of a message show forth. And preachers do this through sermon language, content, and form to support experiencing the gospel in the world today. To this end, preaching that assumes a type of truth that resonates with here and now has a particular texture. Implicitly or explicitly the preacher has to be clear about what hangs in the balance if the message were or were never preached. Clarity here affords the opportunity for imagining the message and its possibilities into the world in concrete ways. Yet this concrete imagining leaves room for the message to take root and sprout beyond the preacher's musings and into the actual life of the community for its own reshaping and imagining.

Preaching for the sake of life forges a sense of connectedness through its immediacy, even in the midst of imaginative resistance to the new possibilities it calls forth. The preacher is aware that they are offering a truth and risking the possibility of getting it wrong. Yet, when the risk of getting it wrong for the sake of life is held against the risk of death if one utters nothing, the preacher chooses to take the risk of getting it wrong.

In these scenarios, the message is not elusive or unattainable, but on the contrary, it is direct and immediate. And the immediacy of the message echoes the deepest hopes and concerns of both God and the people of God. The ultimate litmus test for such a word is in its ability to remain and hold up as *a word* for those who are least honored and recognized in a community. Helping listeners lean into the possibilities of meaningful utterances is all the more important when considering "gospel truth." We must make most plain the need for all to have access to life and thriving over death and demise.

chapter 6
Locating God and Faith on the Ground

In general, a sermon possesses reflections about faith and the faith-story, which is the composition of its God-talk, and these are components listeners anticipate in preaching. For instance, one might anticipate that a sermon will attend to the implicit question, "What does this have to do with faith?" Listeners anticipate hearing something about their beliefs as they pertain to the relationship between God and creation. A narrative about the story of faith and its implications, whether it is cohesive or not, spans a sermon.[1] The primary components in such a narrative typically involve: (1) assumptions about the nature of relationship with the divine, (2) the implications of that relationship for how we move about in the world, and (3) how we relate to one another and the rest of creation. We are not likely to find one consistent and fully developed faith story within a sermon unless a preacher gives particular attention to the way in which their major claims about faith are connected and working units.[2] But rather, we discover a collage of more developed, underdeveloped, and adapted constructions of faith and belief.

With this in mind, multiple assumptions may be present within a sermon at once. For instance, a preacher may convey varying understandings of the relationships between God and humanity. Through preaching we often gain glimpses into a preacher's operative understanding of faith instead of a fully thought-out, organized, or systematic understanding.

These glimpses entail the working, and evolving, framework out of which they speak, live, and promote certain truths about life and God. The participation in God-talk via the sermon happens when we give attention to these working frameworks of faith in both their fragmented and more developed forms.

Aspects of our message, including its here-and-right-now truth, are embedded and connected to these working frameworks of faith. How one develops that which is perceived as truth and God-talk in preaching is mutually linked. Consequently, we demonstrate our understanding of what is true as it relates to God and humanity as we do God-talk. This demonstration involves more than the explicit words we use about faith and this relationship; it also entails the implications one is able to draw from the way in which we cluster ideas and images and color in aspects of faith through preaching.

In the best practices of preaching these implications are cohesive and noncontradictory. For instance, God is not distant and angry in the beginning of the sermon and then benevolent and at hand in the middle of the sermon. This cohesiveness and intentional thought about faith claims is of the utmost importance because haphazard, and sometimes intentionally organized, understandings of faith have led to the exclusion and death of many in the name of God. If God-talk and its images, language, and clustering of ideas have been the very premise of excluding individuals from a community, these same mechanisms must be reconstructed to recover ignored and dispossessed voices. Here I want to be clear that what follows is not a systematic theology for preaching. Instead, I am offering ideas about how we might further develop and expand the working faith claims that take shape on the ground through preaching.[3]

Reconstruction assumes a preacher repurposes claims of a tradition to make better use of their possibilities for a community. The hope is not only to recover ignored and dispossessed voices but also to make space for their full inclusion. Full inclusion includes the ways in which the divine is seen, manifests, and participates in the daily life world of all members of the community. If we do not attend to restructuring faith claims in preaching in this way, then we must own our participation in faith narratives that are proponents of the decay of life instead of its prospering. Our collective understandings of God and faith are (re)created through preaching. And through preaching we have the opportunity to shade and shape our understandings of God and faith with the community.

For those who preach as perceived outsiders there is a clear understanding that "a word from the Lord is needed today," and in such, something is at stake in preaching. Therefore, faith claims that undergird such preaching are concrete and not abstract. Preaching for the sake of life assumes the gospel touches the ground in some way, while it also does the work of translating those touch points to the ground. In a similar manner, preaching for the sake of life assumes the divine presence exists in the here and now. The here and now includes life as it is lived out in its various facets.

The ways in which faith claims are articulated in this approach to preaching connect that which is considered most sacred to the mundane and seemingly ordinary matters of life, as opposed to compartmentalizing it to some areas of life and not others. For instance, the Spirit is just as accessible and present in the commute to work as in the collective worship service. The Holy One is both accessible and an active and participating agent. This connection of the mundane and sacred makes *an utterance from God* accessible, while assuming that a connection to the divine bears particular implications on the day-to-day rhythms of life. Both God and faith are concrete and not abstract.

A Very Present Help

God-talk, alongside its integration with lived wisdom, is one of the primary ways by which the preacher helps make way for sacred-inbreaking. When a community's ways of being are directly confronted by its claims of faith, this provides the space and opportunity for those ways to be shifted, corrected, and pushed to further boundaries. The notion of "in-breaking" assumes a presence entering, interrupting, or invading. All that is holy asserts itself in our here and now. Therefore, there is an understanding that the divine is somehow a participatory agent within and alongside our daily life; likewise, faith is a response through our participation in daily life with the divine. The mundane and ordinary aspects of our existence are opportunities for brushing against a sacred encounter. Preaching itself amplifies this possibility, as it turns up the volume on the presence of the divine in everyday reality—not for some but for everyone in our midst. The best practices of preaching limit the obstacles that obscure both God as active and participating with us and we ourselves as active and participating with God.

God-talk that supports preaching for the sake of life is buttressed by God as a very present helper in and for the purposes of life. And this present helper is the one with whom we participate in the day to day. Faith claims happen when people of faith actually translate the everyday life world as a matter of faith. This translation is often what is missing or where the chasm exists between preaching and the everyday world. If we create divides between the everyday realities of life and faith, then we create an opportunity for the everyday joys and tragedies to be dismissed as irrelevant to that which is at the heart of faith (intentionally or unintentionally). God and faith cannot be out there and strictly otherworldly realities if they are to have any implications on our collective lives together. God is a present help attending to the totality of what it means to be human in an individual way and as people living in community with one another.

(Re)Imaginings of the Ordinarily Sacred

Life with God, life with others, and life as people of faith are interconnected entities. Doing theology through preaching that attends to this interconnectedness requires grounding faith claims in their ordinary implications for both the individual person and the community as they exist in the wider world. The challenge in preaching, especially for those preaching in conversation with dispossessed voices, is to reconnect very personal understandings of faith with communal understandings of faith. This often entails revisiting the meaning of language frequently used, such as that of salvation and redemption.

Locating God and Faith on the Ground

The texture of faith claims that support preaching that conjures life over death assumes an involved God, is relationally oriented, and emphasizes the possibilities of faith and its enactors as resources of help here and now in the everyday. Additionally, such faith claims are textured by attention to opening up possibilities for encountering God and removing unnecessary stumbling blocks for such an encounter, including the engendering of imagery, language for God and humanity, and core tenants of faith that take shape in a sermon.

While the aforementioned are supportive theological frameworks for preaching for the sake of life at hand, a preacher is always in conversations with the traditions of theological frameworks that have shaped a community. Quite possibly, those same traditions have shaped the preacher's outlook. At this juncture, I must own that as I remain in conversation with the women who have faithfully preached us thus far in this book. Here in this chapter, I also push aspects of their articulated faith-stories for the hopes of something more life sustaining for the entire community of God. However, even as I depart from the premises of some of the faith claims, I honor their wisdom for working within the possibilities of tradition for the purpose of negotiating a listening in the face of possible resistance. And we will make use of this wisdom for eliminating both unnecessary stumbling blocks and deadly sentiments that too often cloak our claims about God and faith.

Here exploring black faith and black women's faith narratives brings a particularity to framing faith and God as *a very present help* in preaching. Black faith is not an abstract and ideological project but a lived and enfleshed construction of the faith-story. Kelly Brown Douglas notes the history of a concretized faith and understanding of God in black Christian traditions; she argues that, historically, black people understand God by way of their experiences of God "as they navigated life in a society antagonistic to their very blackness."[4] A core of black faith traditions is that which "advances the life, freedom, and dignity of the black body" as it also fosters spiritual communal and interpersonal relational harmony.[5] Yet, these core theological beliefs that claim faith must be useful and morally connected to black life have often been disrupted and interspersed with contingent beliefs founded in frameworks of body-soul dualism.[6] These dualistic paradigms are the very mechanism that afforded the discarding of black bodies under the white ideological faith project, as they capitalize on what Brown Douglas calls *Platonized Theology*, which frames the body as bad and sinful and the soul as good.[7] When such understandings of the body and soul intersect with the inequities of power within black communal frameworks, it has afforded the historical discarding and subjugation of some black bodies more readily than others.[8]

However, understanding the body as needing to be guarded and disciplined is a complex faith claim when it intersects with the genuine need for safety and protection of black lives in an anti-black world. Such beliefs have also afforded black people the practice of vigilance in where and how their bodies interact with the wider world. Yet the crimes of such claims are felt by black bodies also. They are most keenly felt when they intersect with matters of gender and sexuality that threaten male and heterosexual preferential power. For instance, assumptions about the need of bodies to be guarded and disciplined are what allow women's bodies and queer bodies to be threatened, handled, abused, kept, and disciplined into place, through the guises of due or justified suffering all within frameworks of faith.

When black women and their epistemology and bodily experiences are allowed to interrogate the story of faith and its claims, this has the potential of holding the story of black faith and the faith-story writ large accountable to what Brown Douglas calls a "morally active commitment to advance life, freedom, and dignity for all black bodies."[9] The results are commitments to life, freedom, and dignity that extend well beyond black bodies. Working within paradigms to expand and dismantle historically harmful yet functional claims of faith is a difficult, slow, but necessary task of preaching for the sake of life. For God is *a very present help*, not for some, but for all.

Our preachers offer us an opportunity to see the nature of theological claims that resonate with many, which are claims we cannot afford to leave unattended in preaching if we seek to push the borders of a community's process of thinking and living as people of faith. Such faith claims include ideals of a sovereign and involved God, the nature of relationship with God, and assistance as one moves about in the day to day. These are the faith claims that lead our conversation moving forward; and these claims have framed my considerations for how we effectively expand and further develop our approach to doing theology through preaching by way of understanding how it is taking shape within preaching traditions already.

The Holy One as Sovereignly Involved

An assumption of divine possibility frames faith claims that assert all that is most sacred is a part of the ordinary ins and outs of life. This possibility-type thinking assumes God has the capacity to act and intervene, and part of that capacity is due to the very nature of God being qualitatively different than creation. The Holy is removed and separate from humanity in righteousness, goodness, and power, and is immanently close to lives of humanity—and especially discernable by those who are believers. God is sovereign, involved, and always capable of intervening even if such intervention cannot be predicted in these preacher's stories of faith.

For instance, for Barbara, even as God does not prevent things from happening in a person's life, God is still "a real God that can show up and show out." God does not have constraints within the divine capacity to act, and God performs grandiose interventions on behalf of the children of God and beloved. The children of God are those gathered in her midst. In knowing that God cannot fail, believers must simply "declare the goodness of the Lord and watch God move on (their) behalf. . . . God will lift up a standard against [the enemy]":

> Just *face the enemy, no need to fight him*. And that's not all, when we face our problems. The word tells us in verse 17b not to be afraid or discouraged because *the Lord is with us*. No matter how bad it may look, *God is with you*. He's with you in the chemo treatments, He is with you in the mediation room; He is with you in the unemployment line. He is with you. —Barbara

chapter 6

God is intimately involved in the lives of Barbara and her community as she narrates a relationship in which God is as much sovereign and powerful as God is personal. Barbara removes the aloof "enemy" and "scary situation" and distinctively names them. She declares the presence of God who has the capacity to act in the battle of "chemo treatments," the private thoughts of "mediation rooms," and the instability of the "unemployment line," and to represent those who need provision. God is concerned about, present with, and intervenes on behalf of God's people when they face the tangible "enemy." This God is the same one from whom the preacher brings immediate good news.

In a similar trajectory Patricia very poignantly narrows down the imminence, knowledge, and sovereignty of God during the celebration of her sermon "God in the Midst of the Fire." Patricia's God-talk is steeped in very ordinary statements that pertain to concrete experiences in life. Prior to the moment of celebration, she declares:

> No matter what, God is an on-time God. He may not come when you want him to, but he is always on time. —Patricia

For Patricia, correct timing marks God's intervention. When the immediate act of intervention has not occurred, God is no less present in or knowledgeable of life especially during times of trial. As Patricia says, "God is in the midst of every situation that you are in." And, in the midst of every situation:

> The Lord sees your affliction
>
> The Lord sees your pain
>
> The Lord knows your heartache
>
> The Lord knows your suffering. —Patricia

God is a personal intervening God who acts in correct timing based on supreme knowledge. With supreme knowledge, God acts in concrete ways. Patricia ends her sermon with the affirmation that:

God is a healer

God is a way-maker

God is a lawyer

God is all knowing

Is there anything too hard for God?

There is nothing too big

Nothing too small

Nothing too wide

Nothing too tall that he can't fix

My God, My God! —Patricia

God is sovereign and is all things to those who believe in whatever situation they face. God is one who heals in illness, makes a way amidst obstacles, and provides defense—all with full knowledge. Nothing is too big, unattainable, or undoable for the divine, and this ability can be seen in everyday life matters.

These preachers have an overall understanding of God as sovereign and all-powerful and one who is willing to act on behalf of faithful believers. Interestingly, their tropes of a sovereign and engaged God are overwhelmingly male and masculine in depiction, which exist in contrast to other elements of their sermons that draw upon women's wisdom. In the search of feminine ideals, the greatest interruptions to this masculine identity of God are in the women's use of familiar experience, in which they engage female protagonists with care and bring women's experiences into their sermons for the purpose of their claims about faith (i.e., Teresa's depiction of child birth as power, and Barbara's celebration with fellow sisters of the faith at the great banquet table discussed in chapter 3).

The preachers' articulations about the person of God are not encapsulated in expansive language; but their experiences as women of faith no less shape their understanding that the feminine is a part of and belongs in talk about God, faith, and life. Ultimately, this masculine and sovereign God is not outside of these women's abilities to articulate and understand, as they proclaim the good news and make it plain for those who are listening.

Relational

Relationship is the narrative that undergirds the human connection with divine activity in the world, when one speaks about the realms of possibility for God breaking into the everyday. Assuming the proximity of the presence of God in the world, God's intervening action, or ability to hold creation together, is predicated on connection within the human-divine relationship. Relationship with God is significant for creation, and that relationship has an effect on the relationships within creation.

We often frame faith claims in preaching through some variation of an understanding of such relationship. More traditional faith claims speak about personal knowledge and relationship with God, while other faith claims make intonations about personal knowledge and relationship with God based on how one interacts with and treats one's neighbor. We often hear themes of reconciliation, salvation, and sin as key players in these relational narratives.

Preaching for the sake of life in ways that assume the activity of God also assumes access to relationship with God and accountability in relationship with God, via the direct God-to-human relationship and via what may be viewed as indirect, but no less significant, human-to-human relationship. In this framework the human-to-human relationship reflects one's relationship with God.

Of our preachers, Sharon and Valerie employ the most developed theological language in order to talk about reconciliation within human-to-human relationships as it is connected to human-to-divine relationship. They make use of a tradition that assumes the importance of "personal knowledge" and "personal salvation" while attending to the horizontal implications of that personal knowledge of God. The preachers explicitly link the concern for human relationships to humanity's relationship with God.

For Sharon, God makes a way for wholeness in the human-to-divine relationship via the work, death, and primarily the ascension of Christ. In her sermon "Why We Can't Wait," she states:

> But what this ascension tells us is that in Christ . . . the infinite has embraced the finite. At the very heart of the Trinity now is a human being, Jesus . . . so that we do not wait heaven with a bare hope, but in our Head, Jesus, we already possess it. —Sharon

The human Jesus and the ascended Christ are the means by which Sharon and her community are currently reconciled with God. However, they have the task of "daily sanctification through the help of the Holy Spirit to become more like Christ." As they are "drawn into the family of God" and "profess the faith of being Children of God," they are "mandated to be people of action." In her sermon "Well of Grace," Sharon admonishes that "we must find ways to join the reconciling work of Jesus" even in the extension of grace. Therefore, the woman of John's Gospel who is caught in the act of adultery "is the story of many women—bowed down and hiding because of shame, feeling ugly and unworthy to accomplish God's dreams or any dreams." In extending the work of reconciliation and God's grace, she calls "the church to allow the renewing work of God to flow into the lives of others." This renewing work entails serving the God in very concrete ways by serving others even when it does not "look right" to onlookers, such as "opening the door" and accepting the "nine year-old pregnant girl."

There is little differentiation between Sharon's expressed God-talk on a personal level and that of the other preachers. Sharon communicates a very personal knowledge of separation from God due to sin, and an extremely personal gratitude and awe over reconciliation with God through Christ. Her personal understanding of salvation and redemption affects one's immediate fate and relationship with God in the faith stories of her sermons; these are the same sentiments that the other women express in their focus on human-to-divine reconciliation. How a preacher nuances her understanding of personal relationship with God and its influences on ideas of mission is where the largest differences reside between the preachers.

chapter 6

For Sharon, the experience of personal reconciliation with God does not emphasize conversion for the sake of being made "right" or "righteous"; instead, reconciliation entails an encounter between sin and the sympathetic and accepting grace of a faithful God. Therefore, she engages missional themes around extending a sympathetic and accepting grace to others, as opposed to converting or evangelizing them for the sake of being "made right with God." Empathy leads her ability to imagine the gospel for today.

Valerie places emphasis on God-talk that addresses human-to-human relationships with a different end than Sharon's. Valerie relies on ties of kinship and family grounded in God while focusing on matters of justice. In her sermon entitled "Where's My Daddy," which concerns the status of fatherhood in black communities and the influence of a discriminatory prison system on missing fathers, she states:

> We must proclaim within our community, and beyond its borders, to all of those who understand the Divine kinship of humankind, that the oppressed must go free—now. —Valerie

For Valerie, there is a divine link between human beings that is discernible by some and supports the freedom of those who are dispossessed. Her charge to the gathered community is that, because of this divine kinship, they have a responsibility to proclaim that "the oppressed must go free." Valerie is advocating for a conversion of human relationships. This conversion is literal and tangible: it corrects the discriminatory and false imprisonment that separates black men and children.

Valerie continues her theme of conversion and reconciliation in human relationship in her sermon "To do Justice." She states:

> God's social ideal is a compassionate community in which all persons are equally valued as fellow image bearers. —Valerie

Wholeness in human relationships is synonymous with equality in human relationships, founded in a faith-filled understanding of humanity's connectedness as God's creation and image bearers. For Valerie, "love of God" is inextricably linked "with love for others" in tangible ways.

As she emphasizes justice, she equally emphasizes a personal knowledge of Jesus, which most closely aligns with understandings of salvation and conversion via a faith confession. In Valerie's sermon "He Wants It All," evangelism and justice are intertwined. She challenges those gathered to give their all to God through sacrifice in service to others; in essence, "doing without" in order to give to someone else. However, these sacrificial offerings and deeds that have great implications for righting social and economic injustices hold at their end the opportunity to "win someone to Christ":

> . . . [O]nce we are gone we will be like the women who went to the tomb—it will be too late to do it. The one thing that we will never be able to do in Heaven is to win someone to Christ. I believe we must do what we can, the best we can, all that we can, and when we can. —Valerie

The personal knowledge of Christ and God is of real importance to Valerie. This personal knowledge has been influential in her life and the lives of her listeners; it is the precipitant of their love and actions as they seek wholeness in human relationships. Ultimately, Valerie is communicating that others should experience this personal knowledge through their own conversion experiences as they come to know Christ. Justice in the world and the reconciliation of human relationships are tangible missions because they hold the potential for human beings to experience conversion in God and belonging in "Heaven."

I've made the choice to highlight Valerie and Sharon here because of their pattern to engage both communal and personal concerns in their faith claims about relationship with God. Although not all of the preachers explicitly engage human-to-human relationships as dominant themes within their sermons, it cannot be said that they are unaware of the need for reconciliation in human relationships. Their awareness of injustices and human relational brokenness is evident in the collective memory they draw upon when using familiar experience, as discussed in chapter 3. As opposed to the idea that preachers are oblivious to broken human relationships, it is more plausible that the emphasis on the human and divine relationship is a by-product of faith that heavily relies on the in-breaking of God in the daily lives of believers, particularly when human relationships have failed them.

Collectively Self-Reliant and God-Reliant

One must rely on God when she is disposed of and has been abandoned by human supportive relationships. Therefore, preaching that fills the gap in such lived experiences must mediate the tensions among attending to the need of divine help, reassuring individuals of the divine presence, and holding the community accountable in relationship one to another. An individual, or community, whose hope relies on an intervening act of God gives exhortation that delineates the possibility and presence of such action as a source of help in the day to day. Additionally, such exhortation must also help people sustain hope in the absence of divine intervention or while waiting on divine intervention. The full manifestation of help in this form of preaching does not settle for individual self-reliance in terms of an individual being left to survive for herself; instead, it offers a collective self-reliance in which the community moves in to fill the gaps for individuals.

Preaching for the sake of life assumes divine help as tangible and accessible in the mundane, even when its supernatural manifestation is absent. Black women often carry the burden of mediating the gap between spurring hope in divine possibilities and naming hope in the absence of divine intervention. And we see our preachers' ability to fill this gap of hope as they narrate the presence of hope amidst daily life struggles that largely leave a community reliant on God and reliant on self as a means of survival. Black women's preaching and spiritual traditions offer us possibilities for removing the distance present in some of our imaginings of God and the concrete conditions of life in front of us. Black women have long envisioned Jesus as a friend and helper; and in their referents, they refer to Jesus not as a more mystical Christ alone but as a human being and the personification of an ascended Savior.[10] Likewise, the Spirit, or Holy Spirit, is a persona that is readily accessible as accompaniment and help in life, even if the conditions of life has required one to go it alone.

Cheryl Townsend Gilkes explains a spirit theology as the impetus for the preaching of black women in history.[11] This spirit theology is grounded in the normative and accepted understanding of the Holy Spirit and power of the Spirit within some black faith communities. Historically, within these faith communities there has been an interdependence between the community and the Spirit. The result is that members of the community do not consider the Spirit as a "later appendage" to the Father and Son but as a robust and active persona. Gilkes explains that black women, in their majority membership within black faith communities and their choices of Christian practices, can be considered "agents and advocates for the Holy Spirit or Holy Ghost." In this vein, our preachers' sermons display a history of interdependence between a community and God in a language that has much to do with the abilities of self and God.

Our preachers' existences as black and woman almost require supernatural helpers for a theology that is useful, inspiring, and inciting. They often narrate God as a faithful helper in very imminent ways. For instance, God can literally be a way-maker who will help along the journey of life and faith through means of deliverance and rescue. In her sermon "Are You Your Brother's Keeper?" Patricia's main idea is that human beings should protect and look out for one another; she proclaims, "serving God means you can't help but serve others." Interesting enough, as she exhorts her listeners to serve God by serving others, through the means of collectively self-reliant help, Patricia warns that the only reliable help comes from God:

> You need to be careful who you share your visions and revelations to [with]. People don't always see it as a blessing, some see it as you having something special from God. People are not always happy for you . . . .
>
> People will strip you and try to break you down. But God is your provider, God will make ways out of no way, God can deliver you from anything. —Patricia

Patricia places God's power and sovereignty right alongside divine faithfulness by contrasting the actions of God with the unfaithful actions of people. Although people will forsake others by taking from them and breaking them down, God will give provision and deliverance by making "ways out of no way." God is always faithful; however, people are not and cannot be trusted even as one hopes for being sustained by the community.

As helpers, God, the person of Jesus, and the Spirit are interchangeable in their being named as sources of help and hope. In her sermon "A Stolen Moment," Sharon challenges her listeners to seek and seize the opportunity "to declare what you believe . . . when your back is against the wall." Her premise is that as the thief crucified with Jesus stole the moment to declare his belief in Jesus and ask "remember me when you come into your Kingdom," believers should do the same:

> . . . [I]n a moment in time, what will we say when our backs are against the wall? When we face the loss of careers with good benefits, assisted living and nursing home facilities, become victims of violence, of greed, of addictions, prisoners in ghettos, in old age, in sexism, people with broken bodies, and with broken lives, what will we say? —Sharon

For Sharon, believers are to make declaration of their belief during times of great risk and tragedy, which are the crucifixions of present day. Others include job loss, violence, the abuse of the elderly, greed, and sexism. During these risky circumstances, individuals may be overwhelmed with fear; however, in these circumstances, seeking out others who are not ashamed to declare their belief, along with the support of others who believe, is the means of courage needed to sustain what one believes. The Holy Spirit is the one who helps individuals declare belief in the "redemption purchased by Christ":

> [I]t is the Holy Spirit at work in our lives testifying and applying to us the redemption purchased by Christ by working faith in us . . . It is the Spirit of God that speaks to our hearts saying DO YOU NOT FEAR GOD? —Sharon

The Holy Spirit not only testifies in the lives of believers but also is the source of their ability to declare. The Spirit speaks to hearts, giving individuals strength to testify about belief in God. The Holy Spirit asks "Do you not fear God?" which indicates that to fear God is greater than the fear of risk in declaration. The courage to declare what an individual believes comes from one's reverence of God and the help of the Spirit testifying in their lives.

If God, Jesus, or the Holy Spirit is not named among those who give assistance, the women most often name "self" as the source of help. This self-reliance may seem feasible when it comes to matters of personal piety in terms of individuals being agents of their own help as they seek to know more about God. However, when preachers engage themes of finding or maintaining strength during times of adversity, the struggle and desperation of the "self" remains the viable form of help. Teresa explains to those gathered the process of moving "from pain to power." She explains that in life there are times in which individuals will find themselves "in painful situations not knowing what to do." In these situations, individuals hope for clarity, direction, and spiritual maturity, which will help them "take authority over whatever situation is in front" of them. Prayer is the means of moving from being the victim of a painful situation to having a stronger position in facing a painful situation. Teresa declares that "power comes from pain." However, the arrival of that power is up to the believer herself to facilitate. Teresa likens self-volition to the process of birthing pangs. According to her:

> It is like the birthing process, a woman travailing until she delivers.
> —Teresa

Just as a woman's ability to push and travail is the main precipitant in her birthing a child, so too is the believer's ability to pray and seek God the main precipitant in having the ability to face and live through painful situations. In the birthing room, the assistance of doctors is secondary to the woman and child; however, in the birthing room of life others are secondary to self and God.

When one preaches as an outsider or for the sake of the outsider, we have to determine ways to name the practical demands that calls for one to be both self-reliant and God-reliant in the everyday stuff of life. Yet, we also have to determine ways to help a community and individuals envision an alternative path forward that makes space for tangible helpers in the here and now. These tangible helpers come in the form of human presence and intervention as extensions of divine presence and intervention. If outsider status is determined by one being pushed out of a community or held at bay on its fringes, this is a status of forced isolation that often places unreasonable and unhealthy demands upon an individual—namely, self-reliance unto death. Therefore, God-talk through preaching that recovers those who have been dispossessed names the possibility of divine help and hope in concrete ways—calling the community to enter where the divine would enter.

Self-reliance and spirit-reliance are the by-products of faith steeped in the lived experiences of individuals who have few humanly tangible helpers present. If an individual is marginalized and isolated, she cannot rely upon or guarantee that other human beings will be her helpers. This self- and Spirit-reliant theology in the women's sermons makes sense if we consider the sociocultural history of black women as both black and woman; where, in the absence of excessive human alliances, one has to depend on the intangible-yet-present source for help, assistance, and rescue.

Ingenuity and the Story of Faith

God-talk that supports preaching for the sake of life attends to both the personal and communal aspects of faith. That is, yes, individual faith is of importance, yet individual faith does not exist outside of communal belonging and responsibility. This interrupts practices that have afforded the personal or communal to exist outside of each other. Estranging the communal and personal in theological reflection through preaching has three major risks. First, we risk losing the impulse of communal responsibility and its impact on the daily life of individuals. Second, we risk losing the responsibility of an individual in disturbing the communal equilibrium in ways that makes possible the flourishing of all. And third, we risk losing the very viable and often needed resources that help sustain self-volition and fortitude during difficult, yet inevitable, life circumstances.

Often, when preaching, one contends with understandings of a sovereign divine presence, the connection between personal sin and relationship with that divine presence, and the effect of the former two on day-to-day experiences in life. This might include traditions of preaching that emphasize an all-sovereign and intervening God, whose intervention in the present life world is dependent upon one being in right personal relationship. Historically, these foundations that emphasize right relationship and God's sovereignty have been used to eschew corporate participation in the well-being of individuals, while leaving God and the individual as the primary responsible agents for helping one make it through the day-to-day of life. The narrative goes something along the lines of: My relationship with God dictates God's intervening action in my life, and it is primarily up to God and me to see my way through life.

The consequence of a self-reliant and God-reliant framework is that the community is able to abdicate its responsibility for all individuals thriving within the community. The most dispossessed individual is left as their lone advocate, outside of divine help, in the here and now. Individual strife or suffering is associated with individual shortcomings and personal sin, while such suffering can then be deemed as purposeful or the direct causation of an individual's own infractions.

We are challenged to think in more nuanced ways about suffering, sin, and responsibility considering the realities of what entails the *black thematic universe*,[12] the spectrum of all that lends to black joy and sorrow, and the subsequent intersection of irrational yet long-sustained suffering with black bodies. There must be room to interrogate faith claims via sacred speech that infer or explicitly associate purposefulness in a lack of divine action that lends to suffering or does not prevent it, especially considering the complex interactions of natural circumstances and human agents that lend to unnecessary contradictions in life. Furthermore, the lives of those who are doubly othered—such as black women, as they are pushed to the edges within and outside of their communities—require us to think earnestly about whose suffering and what suffering we deem justified in lieu of our own. There is a constant tension between core and contingent values of faith.

Black womanist and feminist theologians take to task narratives that place value in suffering with intent to make it good and purposeful. We have a history of lived faith on the ground and in texts that assert discipleship means being called to live out and into the literal suffering of the cross. Here, suffering is purposeful as it follows the life of Jesus. The tensions in this framing of purposeful suffering are keenly illuminated when the narrative of Jesus's bodily suffering can be held parallel to the suffering of black bodies throughout history via the crucifixion of chattel slavery, lynching, and their subsequent wounding of black life. The ongoing threat to the lives of many is the idea of Jesus's death being a surrogate, or substitute, for the suffering of someone else. The forced suffering of black women on behalf of someone else has been central to legitimating the ongoing demise of black women, in particular.[13] M. Shawn Copeland argues that the faith claims about suffering are redemptive for black women only in as far as suffering is remembered and produces discomfort and outrage, which continue the movement toward emancipation via resistance.[14]

With this mind, if we remain in conversations with traditions that name salvation and sin, there must be an emphasis on recovering corporate sin and salvation as part and parcel to the gospel, as we work against the violent outcomes of a skewed emphasis on personal sin and salvation. While there are varied ways of correcting this skewed emphasis, the unifying point of departure is the significance of Jesus's life and ministry as his being in solidarity with those who suffer. Although there is tension with retaining narratives of human suffering that attempt to account for purpose in suffering, these motifs are their own legends in our Christian faith traditions. In black Christian traditions in particular, they are tied to a history of a people trying to make sense of the contradictions in life, finding physical solidarity with the crucifixion and resurrection—even though the resurrection ultimately offered life as the final words over suffering and death.

In *The Black Christ*, Kelly Brown Douglas proposes the need for openness that allows for working within traditional faith narratives for the sake of contemporary demands, as we rewrite and replace the symbolism of such narratives.[15] This would involve a claim to Jesus as sustainer, liberator, *and prophet*—one who calls the community to wholeness as it rids itself of all oppression that besets it.[16] Where this work of calling out takes place, so too is the presence of Christ. Crucifixion and resurrection should be retained as a significant part of theological discourse within discussions of our stories of faith—in as far as they literally promote "Life over death—always" as their final conclusions. This is the re-scripting of tradition via the tradition.

Our preachers themselves open up avenues for further explorations of God-talk that incorporate the personal and the communal. If hope in the midst of daily struggle is the major impetus for the overwhelming image of a personally sovereign God, then relationship with God must first be personal before it can be corporate. This is evidenced within Sharon's and Valerie's sermons when they extend a personal knowledge of humanity's relationship to God externally to the purposes of working toward reconciliation in human-to-human relationships. In general, these preaching women are aware of the need for corporate conversion as demonstrated through their engagement with communal memory in chapter 3. However, personal knowledge of a saving and intervening God is the way in which they confront and deal with the daily iterations of collective sin in their daily life struggles of living with faith. Personal knowledge that suffering will not have the last word, as evidenced by Jesus's resurrection, is the means through which the women intonate hope in the midst of unemployment lines, affliction, and the despair of waiting.

The individual paradigm of relationship with God may be taken to an extreme, as previously mentioned, in ways that do not support individual or communal well-being. Instead of rewriting traditional frameworks of faith entirely, there is space for the preacher to make use of these traditional containers to expand their possibilities for experiencing collective life abundant in a community. Namely, the preacher makes use of an existing understanding of God, sin, relationship, and its effect on the everyday to help a community imagine the full possibilities of its faith claims in the ordinary day-to-day. There is room for both personal and corporate understandings of faith to support each other while making straight the path for life to flourish instead of decline. As the preacher uses that with which a community is most familiar she builds bridges to the yet-to-be-imagined or -explored possibilities of belief.

Preaching that explicitly engages faith claims that interrupt the communal–personal dichotomy assumes: Yes, God is a very present help. And as such, there is assurance that where we enter God enters, and where God enters we are called to enter. People of faith have the capacity to be agents of divine interruptions that promote healing and flourishing, just as much as they are dependent on such divine interjections in the everyday. Therefore, yes, my personal responsibility in cultivating relationship with God is significant, while my responsibility in cultivating the holy possibilities for the life of the entire community is just as significant. Personal God-talk and communal God-talk are not mutually exclusive, but mutually dependent. This interdependence prevents the abject terror wreaked on some lives that has been afforded by splits between the personal and communal concerns of God, allowing some to be ignored or discarded at the expense of others.

(Re)Imagining Sermon Development

When doing theology through preaching, the preacher explores ways to make explicit links between the overarching faith-story, the everyday, and an awareness of God on personal and communal levels. God-talk for preaching requires the preacher to determine the theological narrative at work in their message, which is the *overarching faith-story*.

At this point, the content of the narrative is not as significant as being able to articulate an understanding of life with God and life with others. The greater certainty a preacher has about the faith-story being communicated in a message, the better she is able to accomplish the second element of God-talk: relating that larger narrative to concrete experience, or *God in the mundane*. This second element of God-talk entails making loops back to our approach to naming what we perceive to be most true through preaching. This process of naming, as discussed earlier, attends to what we know about the world influencing our understanding about what is most meaningful to us.

Considering the texture of naming truth and its connection to God-talk, attention to concrete experience is not enough. We must attend to concrete experiences of life and the world in ways that address personal and communal aspect of life with God, or *God in the personal* and *God in the communal*. Being attentive to God-talk in this way, further amplifies the location of a sermon's *right here and right now* implications, specifically as it relates to the community's identification as a community of *faith*.

Preaching is not very distinct from other forms of public address and speech without such attention to the faith-story and its implications along the way. But most importantly, vibrant connections between the story of faith people know and the story that pushes the boundaries of what a community can envisage are the impetus for support in the midst of resistance to the gospel's new possibilities for life together.

Overarching Faith-Story

The parallels made among the faith-story, lived experience, and the message are the glue that gives a message contemporary authority and force. If we revisit the practices of our preachers, they demonstrate remarkable similarity in their overarching faith-stories. These stories facilitate both their vision of God's activity in everyday life and the ways in which they narrate God's activity in everyday life. Their descriptions of God in relationship with humanity and humanity's accepting that relationship ensure the certainty of God's action and help in everyday life. There is something at stake in their similar faith-stories—namely, the activity of God in this world and in the life of the believer. Their understanding of God's immanent presence and activity in everyday life parallels the way familiar experience is used to demonstrate the immediacy of their messages' meaning and importance. Their similar convictions about the overarching faith-story influence their similar connections between lived experience and the way their message is conveyed.

Locating the overarching faith-story enables a preacher to define the significance of her message within a theological framework. Reframing the message within the faith-story helps connect concrete experience to the message in ways that ring true and important for people of faith. A preacher's God-talk is reflected in the overall message conveyed and developed within a sermon, but it is not necessarily equal to that message.[17] A preacher's message may reflect a general theological framework that the preacher is narrating their sermon out of, or responding to, without naming or stating that full-blown narrative(s) within the message.[18]

How might this play out in a snapshot on the ground? Let's say I overheard a conversation that inherently devalued children and assumed they are not created equal to adults in the image of God; and then, I am confronted with a text to preach that has children as characters. I may make very intentional efforts to affirm the equal creation of children in the image of God by my choices of stories and the like. I may even paint the child as the main protagonist "who gets it right," without ever referencing either the aforementioned conversation and its underlying assumptions or making my intentions known to listeners. A preacher's use of, engagement with, and association between language and symbols are how one deciphers a sermon's God-talk. And the more a preacher is aware of their God-talk, the better they are able to convey their message in ways that make intentional and coherent associations between both the message and theology.

God-talk can be framed within an understanding of narrative. John McClure explains that, when considered as a narrative, the construction of theology through preaching is closely related to the narrative and symbols of scripture (i.e., God, Christ, humanity, sin, evil, the individual, redemption, and so on as we discussed previously).[19] The loose and more firm associations a preacher makes with ideas of God, sin, redemption, and creation fit into some overarching narrative of the preacher's belief of these concepts in relation to one another. At this point, the meaning of those symbols and their interpretation is not what is important; rather, the ways in which the symbols are arranged in relation to one another in order to create a narrative are paramount.[20] The flow and construction of ideas in relationship to one another are the main focus in attending to narratives of the faith. As the preacher harnesses and becomes more aware of their overarching theological narrative, they are able to better refine it and make more substantive theological claims and associations within the sermon. A sermon's overarching faith-story inevitably influences the content and composition of a preacher's message.

In trying to generate and ascertain the overarching faith-story inferred in a message, a preacher may consider what is being said about life, faith, humanity, and God. Attending to the presence of sin, separation, and opposition within the biblical story, the preacher may then consider what is being inferred about separation from self, separation from others, and separation from God. Now, assuming that God is an active character of the story, the preacher considers what God seeks to offer us, what hinders the reception of what God offers, and what helps us receive what God has to offer. The preacher can then resource the faith-story and fill it out by considering how her or his faith tradition, scripture, and experience interacts with the narrative. In attending to the overarching faith-story, the preacher moves an implicit understanding about the relationship between the divine and humanity into focused view for more intentional engagement.

God in the Mundane

Preaching for the sake of life at hand makes faith-stories concrete. The preacher does not leave the activity of God and God's presence in the abstract; nor is it left to a listener's imagination alone to construct it. This type of preaching makes inroads at naming sin, naming what intervention by God or faith might look like, and naming what faith might look like in everyday life. These movements to name and make explicit do not mean that a preacher's claims lack nuance, that room is removed for listeners making their own connections and final judgments, or that we must have complete certainty about all aspects of God and God's presence. For instance, it may be sufficient to name where the community cannot conceive of God being in the midst of suffering and violence, let's say as the one perpetuating the violence, without having to fully account for the how and where of God's presence.

The most important aspect in naming God in the mundane is the preacher bringing what potentially obscures ideas or jargon of the faith-story (i.e., sin, salvation, redemption, and so on) into the mundane of everyday terms and experiences. This work is of significance because it creates another point of immediate recognition and a familiar place of engagement for listeners while undergirding the concreteness and relevance of the sermon to everyday life experiences. Being able to do God-talk through and with the mundane minimizes the distance between listeners and the authority of the message as it relates to living with God and with others. In short, make the faith-story concrete.

We construct meaning through the association or disassociation between things in our everyday words and experiences. Tisdale offers that, in preaching, this construction of meaning is not *ex nihilo*, out of nothing, but is facilitated in a metaphorical way by placing objects beside one another that may not have previously existed side by side (i.e., the biblical text and the congregational context, or faith and continuing to believe even as one lacks resources).[21] Within this bilateral dance of two objects, the imagination is engaged and meaning is created. This dance is what is at work in the idea development of the preacher,[22] and it is also at work with the mundane, which is used as a means of doing God-talk.

Renaming and reassigning the faith-story through everyday words and associations helps locate and construct theological meaning in ways that remain in close proximity to lived experience. If the meaning implicit in the symbols and narratives of the biblical story are aloof due to the distance of those narratives from lived experiences, then finding symbols closer to lived experience brings meaning into closer proximity for the community. The push here is for the translation of the narrative of scripture and the theological arc of the text; this particular translation entails the narrative of scripture being translated into the everyday words and associations of the experiences of listeners. Within this proximity to lived experience is the place wherein the community is able to see the God who acts in the Bible as the same God acting on their behalf. This is the work of making it plain.[23]

For a preacher to begin mining the everyday and mundane experience of this world as a means for communicating theological meaning and significance, they may start with simply making loose associations with the words and concepts identified in the original faith-story. This would entail placing each word, short phrase, or concept in isolation on a page and writing down beside that word the first images, words, and scenarios that come to mind. After making these associations, one might step back from the page and try to reconstruct the overarching faith-story based on the words on the page. The alternative would be to simply rewrite the overarching faith-story several times until something recognizable and synonymous with concrete experience arises. The final step comes in the process of implementing these ideas into the sermon. The hope is that the preacher is able to better narrate the overarching faith-story and better narrate everyday experiences into the overarching faith-story.

Often, when helping a preacher develop a message or reconstruct a message, I run into theological terms that are never defined but repeated over and over again. For instance, the term *sin* will come up several times, without any substantial indication of what it signifies in that particular message, how it takes shape, and what it looks like. The same might be true for words such as *redemption, reconciliation, faith*, and the like. Locating faith in the very ordinary for the sake of sermon development pushes the preacher not to "hide" their message behind blanket terms but to translate, specify, and be clear for the purposes of the message at hand.

The Faith-Story & the Mundane: An Example

In finding God in the mundane, a preacher turns to determining where and how the overarching faith-story of the sermon can be identified in everyday lived experience. The following narrative is a demonstration of translating the overarching faith-story into the mundane:

> God seeks to give humanity abundant life. Sin hinders us from receiving that abundant life.

Doing God-talk by way of the mundane would need to concretize each of these somewhat vague and distant concepts (i.e., abundant life, sin) within the everyday experiences and associations of the community's life. For instance, if sin hinders us from receiving the abundant life God offers, the next step is to concretize abundant life and sin. Locating God in the mundane may consist of the following narrative:

chapter 6

Abundant life is safety, love, and provision in all areas of our lives. Sin and the opposition to that abundant life is the reality of greed by a few individuals taking more than needed, the threat of violence that occurs in abuse, and the lack of love for one's self.

But our narrative is still lacking. Hope is present not only in God's gift of abundant life but also in the help offered to receive the abundant life in the presence of that which seeks to hinder it. This identification of help traces back to how and where our preachers communicated help in this world and in the struggle for living with God. As they relied primarily on themselves and God for help in this world and in the struggle of life and faith, the certainty of help was the catalyst of hope and inspiration. The concretization of hope is help and assistance in moving toward the mark that has been set in a message. Our "God in the mundane" narrative lacks the aspect of help because our original faith-story lacked the aspect of help. Hope identified in help offered to receive the gift of God's abundant life could be any of the following and more, depending on the preacher's theological beliefs:

> Others hold us accountable in their willingness to intervene and confront our lack of self-love, safety, and provision, through concrete plans for safety, rescue, and rehabilitation; particularly when we have jeopardized our well-being by engaging in activities and relationships that do not affirm our value as human beings and that place our emotional and physical well-being in jeopardy.

or

> The Spirit strengthens and enables us to overcome greed in our resources and to be a part of the community's pursuit of life abundant as we provide food for those without food, shelter for those without shelter, and medical services for those who cannot afford medical care.

Again, the sentences above may never appear in the sermon, but instead are the guiding frameworks for how we make determinations about what material to include in a sermon in order to "show" listeners why our claims are significant matters of faith.

God in the Personal

As one attempts to link the faith-story to everyday words and associations there are additional steps to consider. The additional step is our ability to connect personal knowledge of God to the overarching faith narrative. This connection of God to the personal entails finding the spaces in which individuals may explicitly name their experience of the divine and then find their location within the story. Engaging the personal through this additional point of connection creates a means of framing the theological significance of a message. Similar to the effect of mining personal experiences for the purpose of conveying the thematic claims of a sermon, the presence of personal connections in God-talk makes possible an additional point of accessing the possibility of truth that a message proposes.

Connecting God-talk to the personal is of significance because it recalls to memory qualitative encounters with that which is narrated as holy, even as it creates opportunity for such encounters. As it has been espoused about the hopes of preaching in general, and as we place those hopes in conversation about black preaching traditions in practice—the search and excavation of scripture does not hold scripture as the idol sought after; instead, an encounter with God is what is sought in the engagement of scripture and, conversely, in the preaching moment. We encounter the God who wants to be known and who self-reveals within our concrete ways of knowing.

Preaching opens space for a community or person to access their knowledge of God through the memory of tangible encounters or experiences, even as it facilitates new or expanded ways of understanding God and faith. Shaping the story of faith through preaching is not simply about the meaning constructed through signs and symbols, but about limiting obstacles as we create paths to points of connection and identification with the story of faith and the activity of God around us.

Attending to faith and its connection to personal ways of knowing through preaching is carried out in different ways across traditions, as it responds to differently determined interests and needs of a community. Yes, listeners expect to connect with preaching via their lived wisdom and experiences; however, the texture of that connection varies. For instance, this search for the personal could be influenced by stark divides between "sacred" and "secular" domains of life, purporting that there is no genuine place for both the political and the social within church and communities of faith.[24] Here the personal emphasis would manifest as a heavy emphasis on personal piety and practice. The search for the personal may also arise from the genuine search and need for a personal and accessible God in the everyday struggle for life as one is forced to the edges of society.[25] Whether the personal is present in preaching by the division of sacred and secular or by the struggle for survival—be it both/and or neither/nor—its presence is a point of connection and is often sought by listeners.

How the preacher attends to those expectations with integrity is of our primary concern. When finding God in the personal, being able to tell the story is of significance while incorporating the overarching faith-story and personal encounters within the narrative. The starting point for the preacher's imagination has to include one remembering their own point of entry in the overarching faith-story. Just as the preacher is the first recipient of the message, they are also the first one shaped by the message. For this reason, locating God in the personal encounter of the preacher is just as significant as the preacher being apprehended by the message before it is offered to others. The direct questions the preacher poses to understand where they enter the story include: Where have I known and understood God or faith in this way? Where have I known and understood opposition and sin, and help and hope in this way? Again this is the preacher's starting place for questioning and imagining but not the final resting place.

In locating God in the personal outside of self, a preacher may consider imagining the faces of specific individuals and what their personal encounters with the divine may be or have been within the faith-story. This is similar to the way in which the personal is pursued in creating mutual experiences through imagining the individual. For example, where does the battered spouse encounter God or God encounter the battered spouse in this narrative? What about the abuser? The child? What about the person struggling to survive? Or the person without a care in the world? For the hope is not to end with the preacher's experience, but to use this imagining as a launch pad to imagine with and on behalf of listeners.

Our ability to imagine implications beyond ourselves helps listeners place faith in conversation with their lives, but it also helps move personal knowing to the next steps. This movement has implications for our accountability and responsibility to that knowing and for our relationship with others.

God in the Communal

Engaging the story of faith and its implications in community with others strengthens the "at-stake" aspects of a message and its proximity to what it means to live life with God and with others. More explicitly, uniting the personal and communal affirms that there is something significant about faith and the gospel beyond the individual and affirms that within the communal framework, faith does not exclude individual bodies by absorbing them indiscriminately into a group or by pushing them to the fringes of a group. This connection between the personal and communal is demonstrated in the history of some black preaching traditions during the civil rights movement of the 1960s. Because of their personal-private understandings of faith, some communities moved outward in action based on the inherent social-corporate implications of the gospel.

Those primarily responsible for teaching within faith communities are key in reshaping the private-personal and social-corporate theological discourses in relationship to one another. As a preacher depicts a very particular theological worldview, over time they also promote within the community a very particular theological worldview—be it consciously or subconsciously.[26] There is often an uneven presence between social and personal concerns of faith in preaching. Personal faith talk either outpaces and takes over social and corporate aspects, or social faith talk absorbs the personal and private aspects. For many communities, the former is the more frequent occurrence, while often the latter is common in communities that identify themselves as white mainline progressives. The hope is for our methods of preaching and teaching to probe the social-corporate and personal-private dimensions as practical aspects of faith talk, not as an occasional endeavor but a constant one.[27]

At this point, the question becomes: How do those who are primarily responsible for education in faith communities (and this includes preachers) participate in more even treatments of both private and social dimensions of interpretation and faith. Connecting to suffering and recognizing the suffering of others provides a lens for helping move our preaching along the continuum from the inward focus of the personal to the outward focus of the other.[28] This includes moving between up-close encounters with both the private suffering and the collective suffering we witness in our midst, and then moving toward those same encounters in up-close biblical study, preaching, and general conversation—not moving away from them.

Unfortunately, in my experience we are not as likely to open our hearts and minds to the suffering or even the joys of someone else, especially one whom we deem most unlike ourselves, until we find points of alignment with the joy and suffering we ourselves have known. And the preacher's task is that of helping bring those synergistic points into our purview. The work requires intention as the preacher creates flickers back and forth between what one personally knows and what one has never experienced. For instance, if one preaches in a community or amidst a momentary group of listeners who are resistant to discussing the alarming rates of death of black people by violent means in both private encounters and at the hands of local and federal law enforcement officers, multiple things must occur before any movement toward a collective sense of responsibility happens in attending these issues. The preacher must first find a way to help those gathered name premature death as traumatizing and heart wrenching. However, naming it as heart wrenching is not enough; it must then be named as what defies the hopes of God for life abundant. Only then can the preacher discern with and help the community find its means of responding to such tragedies as a part of their being accountable to the faith claims they espouse. The gateway to this movement from resistance or indifference to empathy and action is the ability to draw upon what listeners know about their own experiences of loss or imaging of what their loss might feel like.

Ultimately, as a preacher seeks to extend the personal of God-talk to the communal, their attention must include considering the implications of one's own responsibility to others based on a knowledge of and experience of faith. The preacher should consider where "the other" enters the faith-story, what the particular faith-story may mean for the world in which we live, who benefits from the story, who is counted as insignificant within it, and what kind of response the faith-story requires from the community of faith.

IN PRACTICE
Naming God and Faith

Reflecting on God-talk is helpful both in the initial creative process and as a tool of analysis after the sermon is developed and determined to be pulpit ready. Here are some practical steps to help jumpstart your reflection:

1. *Overarching Faith Story:* In consideration of the message, what do you desire to be described about life, faith, humanity, and God in this message? Jot down your responses as they come to you in complete or incomplete phrases, images, or ideas.

2. *Overarching Faith Story:* Now consider what is being inferred about separation from self, separation from God, and separation from others in this message?

3. *God in the Mundane:* Go back to words and ideas formulated in brainstorming the overarching faith-story. Jot down and say aloud the first thoughts, words, images, and ideas that come to mind as you attend to each idea or word.

4. *God in the Mundane:* Now move back from the page and your brainstorming. Lay them aside. Try to rewrite or reconstruct your overarching faith-story based on the new words, phrases, and images on the page.

5. *God in the Personal:* Where do YOU enter this faith-story?

6. *God in the Communal:* Where do other people entre this faith-story? And where do those deemed "other" enter this faith-story?

7. Now, rewrite the faith-story in a way that seeks to account for your exploration and discoveries in "God in the mundane," "God in the personal," and "God in the communal."

Attending to God-talk in sermon development helps us determine not only what is at stake in our message but also what is theologically at stake and of significance *about* the message. If nothing can be claimed as significant as a matter of faith, then the message has missed the opportunity to ring clear and true as a word from the Lord for today. When our conceptualization of the overarching faith-story in our sermons is robust, we are better able to engage and utilize scripture, the message we hope to communicate, and the lived wisdom of those in our midst for the sake of a right here and right now message.

Sacred Storytelling

Faith claims made *within* preaching are distinct yet not disconnected from our attempts to articulate understandings *about* preaching as a faith practice. We often have an underdeveloped or contradictory story of faith at work within our sermons. For giving attention to "how" to tell the story of faith itself is underdeveloped in our conversations about the craft of preaching. Claims about faith made through preaching both echo backward to a community's history and shape the ripples of its future. Yet, until we interrogate the faith claims within our preaching, we do not fully attend to the implications of our message as it lands within the community of faith.

What we say explicitly or implicitly about faith through preaching overtime has enduring effects on a community of faith, including its growth or malformation. Locating what is most sacred in the mundanely personal and communal of everyday life affords the greatest opportunity to shrink the gaps between those expositions of faith that force some to the uttermost parts of a community and those expositions of faith that bring our lives together and move more in harmony with a gospel that posits abundant life for all. If we are not doing this sacred storytelling, then we are not truly doing the work of claiming the story of faith through preaching.

conclusion
Risk-Taking for the Sake of Life

Preaching does not exist for the sake of itself. It is a creative practice and exists for the hopes of something more. We urge preaching alongside its holy hopes to make way for sacred reverberations in our communities and world. Preaching hopes to render evident what is most true and holy—namely, proclamation that is recognizable by the entire community, as it possesses contemporary veracity and sustains the lives of those gathered. A message that makes way for such possibilities has the potential to reshape and push a community forward in a holistic manner.

Preaching is a work of sacred imagining that requires divine presence. However, preaching also relies upon the work, history, and presence of a community. A community has the ability to state what is and what is not preaching. The gathered community affirms that "preaching" and proclamation are taking place. And it does this work of affirmation in conversation with tradition, biases, and assumptions about the ways in which holy truth rings true. The gathering community can shout such reverberations by the same tradition, biases, and assumptions.

Preaching closes in on itself when the blueprints established by a community become fixtures that are not fluid. Through rigidity preaching can limit possibilities. Just as a road sign is intended to point in a direction for the purposes of moving traffic along a particular route, so also is the hope of preaching. Preaching is never a fixture intended for the purposes of itself; instead it facilitates the movement on to something more. The community misses an opportunity when preaching becomes rigid while focusing most on its sound, content, performance, and aesthetics as they are carried out by the particulars of whose body shows up to preach. We close ourselves off from the possibility of life anew.

The intonations of *the outsider* filtered through preaching holds the possibility to force a community to move beyond reinforcing road signs for the sake of road signs. The voice of the one who dares to move in foolish courage reminds us that preaching is forever influx and was never intended to be one thing in shape or form. Instead, preaching is a practice that demands fluidity for the sake of its own aims in the midst of a community—namely, the community's flourishing and life itself.

There are new possibilities as the continuation of preaching, the proclaimer, and the community become a triad in determining the shifting road markers. In best practices, the three work in harmony to bear witness to an experience that holds the potential of healing, giving new life, and reorienting—*proclamation*. Proclamation gives space and reconnects a community in ways that subvert othering. Preaching that facilitates proclamation resembles that which proclamation makes possible; it builds connections instead of divisions, opens a community up instead of closing it off, aims for restoration instead of depletion, and makes room for more of creation's flourishing.

Leaving Space for Possibilities

We need to push our assumptions about preaching in relationship to black women in particular. Yet, this by no means ascribes what authentic preaching by black women *cannot* be. Just as much as black preaching must not be described entirely by a cultural narrative and stereotype of the tradition, we must guard against saying that women, womanhood, and femininity do not perform with affinities to traditional imagining of black preaching. A woman can whoop and be fully charismatic in her preaching, having more affinities with the historically codified description of black preaching. And a woman can deliver and perform a sermon completely otherwise and still render a valid sermon within black preaching traditions. If we do not leave space for such possibilities we simply reinforce racist and sexist assumptions about gender and preaching.

The issue is not preaching being "black," "like a man," or "like a woman." The troublesome manner is our tendency to label such an expression of preaching as being "like a man," "like a woman," or not. Our imaginings have been overwhelmingly stifled by a default imagery of maleness and what masculinity looks like alongside whiteness; and in turn, anything that moves in contradiction to such imaginings is inherently deficient. As we uncouple our marking of legitimate preaching practices from the gendered and racial stereotypes that enshroud them, we more faithfully affirm a variety of preaching practices within a community and allow preaching to take on its fullest potential in our midst. This uncoupling is not the same as erasing cultural or even bodily distinctions. Instead, we are in search of greater multiplicity in cultural practices of preaching.

Cultivating Risk-Taking for Ingenuity

Wherever we find ourselves in community, we constantly negotiate the expectations of that community. We move within and around the confines of the structures we inherit. Many minoritized bodies choose to remain in contexts that have not been hospitable to their presence, historically, and at times have been downright hostile. Granted these are not the only options. One may determine it is best to use their voice elsewhere, which is a valid decision. Those who remain and render a message in places that would prefer their invisibility, dare to preach with a distinct and creatively tactical imagination for the sake of their deepest convictions—*ingenuity*.

Preaching is an act of risk-taking that relies on ingenuity. The practice is ultimately a risk we take for the sake of life as it hangs in the balance. We constantly risk getting it wrong for the sake of getting it more right. We risk going into the unknown territory of the pulpit itself, the bidding of sacred texts, a message yet to be discerned, and a sermon yet to be received. Black women have often been left to discern and intuit these risks alone. This holy risk-taking is carried out in isolation due to the many *man-made* obstacles that limit mentors and models, erase their preaching *herstories*, and block paths from pew to pulpit. Yet, they take the holy risk and preach.

Risk-taking is preceded by vulnerability and courage. Preaching is an act of doing, being, and thinking, all while deeply discerning, intuiting, and listening. The work is vulnerable as we move in and out of our deepest ways of knowing for the sake of *a word from the Lord for today*. Vulnerable and courageous work requires the same in preparation. Sermon preparation is not first concerned with what we think is "right" or "wrong" or with having "the answer." Preparation is shaped by a courageous pursuit of unknown possibilities that have not yet rang fully clear and true. Sermon development is a process of ultimate discovery. This discovery is led by our deepest ways of knowing as a person of faith trying to reconcile the joys and sorrows of life with who we believe we all are most created to be.

Preach, *Regardless*.

There is no partial inclusion or creation in the *kin-dom* of God. However, our means of *othering* constantly attempt to name some of us as partially or unequally created in the *imago Dei*—in the image of God. And this process wreaks havoc in the lives and on the literal bodies of persons in our midst. Those who live under the assault of being othered have a different demand placed upon their preaching ministries, as they search out the yet-to-be-made-possible. This demand requires nuanced risk-taking for the sake of their lives and ultimately the life of their entire community.

Every sermon is an act of risk-taking if we—every preacher, *outsider* or not—are faithful in our preaching ministries. For we are attempting to say something fully life sustaining in a world that often affirms death over life. Before we can ever take such a risk, we ourselves have to believe that something more is possible and that it is a holy possibility demanding a holy risk. Until this day, there will always be an *outsider* daring to preach. And to you, we all say, "Preach, *regardless*."

notes

Introduction: #PerceivedOutsider

1. See "#SayHerName," African American Policy Forum, http://www.aapf.org/sayhername/.

2. Anthony Pinn offers the black *labyrinth* as an alternative descriptor for the porous, multidimensional, and continuous embodied aspects of global black life (see Anthony B. Pinn, "Introduction: The Black Labyrinth, Aesthetics, and Black Religions," in *Black Religion and Aesthetics: Religious Thought and Life in Africa and the African Diaspora*, ed. Anthony Pinn (New York: Palgrave Macmillan, 2009), 2–4.

3. See Toni Morrison, *The Origin of Others* (Cambridge: Harvard University, 2017).

1. When Bodies and Unimaginative Practice Collide

1. In *White Women's Christ, Black Women's Jesus*, Grant argues that the historical realities of slavery and black women in domestic service most adequately demonstrate the intersectionality of realities of race, gender, and class in the lives of black women (see Jacquelyn Grant, *White Women's Christ and Black Women's Jesus: Feminist Christology and Womanist Response*, American Academy of Religion Academy Series [Atlanta: Scholars Press, 1989], 6). Black feminist criticism has also noted the systematic social

control over the lives and imaging of black women based on economic, political, and ideological dimensions. Such social control has consisted of assigning black women a subordinate place in the world, defining stereotypes, and showing their erasure from the body politic. This includes their imagining as mammy, Jezebel, mother, breeder, and outright invisibility (see Patricia Hill Collins, *Black Feminist Thought: Knowledge, Consciousness, and the Politics of Empowerment*, rev. 10th ed. [New York: Routledge, 2000], 4–5; and Hortense J. Spillers, "Mama's Baby Papa's Maybe: An American Grammar Book," chap. 8 in *Black, White, and in Color: Essays on American Literature and Culture* [Chicago: University of Chicago Press, 2003]).

2. Hortense J. Spillers explains African American women exist as a different female gendered being than women of the dominant culture as it relates to their presence in American discourse and history. This is primarily due to the influences of oppression as it relates to their race, placing them outside of traditional symbols of female gender, making them a "different social subject" (see Spillers, "Mama's Baby Papa's Maybe").

3. See Bettye Collier-Thomas, *Daughters of Thunder: Black Women Preachers and Their Sermons, 1850–1979*, 1st ed. (San Francisco: Jossey-Bass, 1998).

4. In her 1984 book *Sister Outsider*, Audre Lorde discusses how "in a patriarchal power system, where white-skinned privilege is a major prop, the entrapments used to neutralize black women and white women are not the same." Also, she continues to explain the mislabeling of black women as "anti-Black" when they are expressing "anti-sexist" sentiments in the battle against "racial erasure" that both black women and men face (see Audre Lorde, *Sister Outsider: Essays and Speeches* [Berkeley: Crossing Press, 2007], 118–20).

5. See Cheryl Gilkes, *If It Wasn't for the Women: Black Women's Experience and Womanist Culture in Church and Community* (Maryknoll, NY: Orbis Books, 2001); Marcia Riggs, *Plenty Good Room: Women Versus Male Power in the Black* Church (Cleveland, OH: Pilgrim Press, 2003); Cheryl Gilkes, "There Is a Work for Each One of Us: The Socio-Theology of the Rev. Florence Spearing Randolph," chap. 9 in *How Long This Road: Race, Religion, and the Legacy of C. Eric Lincoln*, ed. Alton B. Pollard and L. H.

Whelchel (New York: Palgrave Macmillan, 2003), 131–34; and Delores C. Carpenter, "A Time to Honor: A Portrait of African American Clergywomen," chap. 10 in *How Long This Road*.

6. For more on black women, preaching, and religious life, see Teresa L. Fry Brown, *Weary Throats and New Songs: Black Women Proclaiming God's Word* (Nashville: Abingdon Press, 2003); Bettye Collier-Thomas, *Daughters of Thunder: Black Women Preachers and Their Sermons, 1850–1979*; Chanta M. Haywood, *Prophesying Daughters: Black Women Preachers and the Word, 1823–1913*; Evelyn Brooks Higginbotham, *Righteous Discontent: The Women's Movement in the Black Baptist Church, 1880–1920* (Cambridge, MA: Harvard University Press, 1993); and Marcia Riggs, *Can I Get a Witness? Prophetic Religious Voices of African American Women: An Anthology* (Maryknoll, NY: Orbis Books, 1997).

7. This is a play on the title of the edited volume by Akasha (Gloria T.) Hull, Patricia Bell-Scott, and Barbara Smith entitled *All the Women Are White, All the Blacks Are Men, but Some of Us Are Brave: Black Women's Studies* (New York: The Feminist Press at CUNY, 1982).

8. See Patricia Hill Collins, *Black Feminist Thought*, 25.

9. Roxanne Mountford discusses the contested rhetorical spaces of the pulpit in American Protestantism and the conceptualization of preaching and its rhetoric as a "manly art" (see Mountford, *The Gendered Pulpit: Preaching in American Protestant Spaces, Studies in Rhetorics and Feminisms* [Carbondale: Southern Illinois University Press, 2003]).

10. Preaching as a historical practice shapes the structures of its continuation and those structures postulate power. Preaching is both a product of environments and their histories and a tool by which bodies of difference engage their environments. For more on practices, their questioned adoption, and the role of the body in that adoption, see Pierre Bourdieu, *Outline of a Theory of Practice*, trans. Richard Nice, *Cambridge Studies in Social and Cultural Anthropology*, (Cambridge: Cambridge Press, 2007), 71, 94.

11. Every performance of masculinity does not count and is not recognized within the historical image of the black preacher. One has to note

the intersection of sexuality and the performance of masculinity as they relate to the male bodies who are historically allowed to occupy pulpit space in black worship spaces and those who are restricted from pulpit space but readily accepted as ministers of worship or music. Alisha L. Jones attends to the perceived performance of masculinity and sexuality as it takes shape within black worship spaces, specifically that of music ministries, and the limits of such performativity in perceived spaces of authority such as the pulpit (see Alisha L. Jones, "Are All the Choir Directors Gay? Black Men's Sexuality and Identity in Gospel Performance" in *Issues in African American Music: Power, Gender, Race, & Representation*, ed. Portia K. Maultsby and Mellonee V. Burnim [New York: Routledge, 2017], 216–35).

12. The image of the black preacher has some continuity with the "slave preacher"; likewise, the slave preacher's notable characteristics have continuity with characteristics of prominent black preachers during the twentieth-century civil rights era. The ability to both control and incite resistance was rooted in the preacher's rhetorical prowess often alongside his illiteracy. The marks of leadership, communication, and rhetorical prowess exhibited by the slave preacher can be identified with prominent public preacher figures such as Martin Luther King, Jr., and Malcolm X, whose ministries sparked larger societal interest in black preaching and homiletical discourse. We also see etchings of the image of the black preacher in film and art, which further solidify this image of a cultural product that is continually signified on and reinscribed. For more on the image of the black preacher, see Benjamin Albert Botkin, *Lay My Burden Down: A Folk History of Slavery* (Athens: University of Georgia Press, 1989); H. Beecher Hicks, Jr., *Images of the Black Preacher: The Man Nobody Knows* (Valley Forge, PA: Judson Press, 1977); and James Weldon Johnson and Henry Louis Gates, *God's Trombones: Seven Negro Sermons in Verse*, rev. ed. (New York: Penguin Books, 2008).

13. Pierre Bourdieu proposes that environments produce systems and durable strategies that are collectively orchestrated without being the product of the orchestrated actions of a conductor (see Bourdieu, *Outline of a Theory of Practice*, 72).

14. Katie Cannon argues that through ingenuity black women create a set of values that are more than those imposed on them; as moral agents, they discern genuine choices on their own terms for living in the here and now, and these possibilities are sources of hope (see Katie Cannon, *Black Womanist Ethics* [Eugene, OR: Wipf & Stock, 2006], 44, 161).

15. Practice theories distinguish between those actions that are *strategies* and those that are *tactics*. Michel de Certeau describes a strategy as the postulation of power; whereas a tactic is the absence of strategic power and specifically the "art" of the system's *weak* and the means by which individuals "make do." The system's *weak* is Certeau's descriptor of those with less power. Preaching itself is made up of strategies that have been established over time. As preaching is engaged by minoritized bodies, it has potential as a tactical means of asserting one's agency and personhood over and against the same systems that have excluded them from preaching (see Michel de Certeau, *The Practice of Everyday Life*, trans. Steven Rendall [Berkeley: University of California Press, 1984], xix, 37–38).

16. I have written elsewhere about the expansion of communal preaching practices as a result of the tactical expression of individual agency through preaching. See Lisa Thompson, "'Now That's Preaching!': Disruptive and Generative Preaching Practices," *Practical Matters* 8 (March 2015), http://practicalmattersjournal.org/2015/03/01/now-thats-preaching/.

17. Evelyn Parker, "Womanist Theory," in *The Wiley Companion to Practical Theology*, ed. Bonnie J. Miller-McLemore, 1st ed. (Hoboken, NJ: Blackwell, 2012), 204–5.

18. Teresa Fry Brown, "An African American Woman's Perspective: Renovating Sorrow's Kitchen," in *Preaching Justice*, Christine Smith, ed. (Minneapolis: Wipf & Stock, 1998).

19. Ibid.

20. Donna E. Allen, *Toward a Womanist Homiletic: Katie Cannon, Alice Walker, and Emancipatory Proclamation* (New York: Peter Lang, 2013).

21. Delores S. Williams names such moments along a continuum of quasi-womanist and genuine-womanist fragments. Quasi-womanist

fragments are those that offer a partial inclusion of the feminine, black womanhood and girlhood, and the family, while genuine-womanist fragments are "totally inclusive" of the mosaic that makes up the community (see Delores S. Williams, "Rituals of Resistance in Womanist Worship," in *Women at Worship: Interpretations of Northern American Diversity*, ed. Marjorie Procter-Smith and Janet R. Walton [Louisville: Westminster John Knox, 1993], 216–18).

22. Engaging the sermons of black women first as expressions of ingenuity locates value in their productions without designating how their productions "should" function. Value is in the act of black women preaching, regardless of where their preaching is located on the continuum of accommodation and resistance. Here, the highlight and emphasis is on agency or the capacity to act. Saba Mahmood asserts: "Agentive capacity is entailed not only in those acts that resist norms, but also in the multiple ways in which one inhabits norms" (see Saba Mahmood, "Agency, Performativity, and the Feminist Subject," in *Bodily Citations: Religion and Judith Butler*, ed. Ellen T. Armour and Susan M. St. Ville, [New York: Columbia University Press, 2006], 186).

23. Marla Frederick has engaged similar ideas of creativity and agency as they relate to the spirituality of black women. She explains that creativity in the midst of struggle is both resistance and black women's utilization of agency. Such premises are in direct contrast to black women's religiosity being labeled as an opiate that continues to produce submissive and disengaged individuals who participate in their own oppression. These women creatively inhabit the norms of black religious life, expressing agentive capacity as their spirituality influences their engagement in the public and private spheres of everyday life (see Marla Frederick, *Between Sundays: Black Women and Everyday Struggles of Faith* [Berkeley: University of California Press, 2003], 8–10).

24. In *Weaving the Sermon*, Christine Smith brings to the center of homiletic theory the authority of women's experiences as a weft that can transform tradition and preaching (see Christine Smith, *Weaving the Sermon: Preaching in a Feminist Perspective* [Louisville: Westminster John Knox Press, 1989]).

25. Ellen Davis describes imaginative precision in preaching for the sake of a message that is true in the face of a genuine need within the community (see Ellen Davis, *Wondrous Depth: Preaching the Old Testament* [Louisville: Westminster John Knox, 2005], 68–72).

26. See Richard Lischer, *The End of Words: The Language of Reconciliation in a Culture of Violence* (Grand Rapids: Wm. B. Eerdmans, 2005), 45.

2. Ingenuity for the Sake of Proclamation

1. For more on sermon as genre and its rhetorical strategies, see John S. McClure, *The Four Codes of Preaching: Rhetorical Strategies* (Louisville: Westminster John Knox Press, 2003).

2. James Nieman attends to the significance of understanding the aim of a practice in connection with preaching as a specific practice, stating, "A specific practice never exists to repeat or perpetuate itself, even if performed with great skill or excellence. Meaningful practices push past any admiration of emulation to implement ends beyond themselves." Here my argument is that the hoped-for aim is proclamation itself (see James Nieman, "Why the Idea of Practice Matters," chap. 2 in *Teaching Preaching as a Christian Practice: A New Approach to Homiletical Pedagogy*, ed. Thomas G. Long and Leonora Tubbs Tisdale [Louisville: Westminster John Knox Press, 2008], 28).

3. See H. Beecher Hicks, *Images of the Black Preacher: The Man Nobody Knows* (Valley Forge, PA: Judson Press, 1977), 19.

4. Ibid., 19, 105.

5. Ibid., 11.

6. Zora Neale Hurston, *Jonah's Gourd Vine: A Novel* (New York: Perennial Library, 1990).

7. Ibid., xi.

8. See Henry Mitchell, "African American Preaching," in *Concise Encyclopedia of Preaching*, ed. William H. Willimon and Richard Lischer

(Louisville: Westminster John Knox Press, 1995); Henry H. Mitchell, *Black Preaching: The Recovery of a Powerful Art* (Nashville: Abingdon, 1990); *Celebration and Experience in Preaching*, rev. ed. (Nashville: Abingdon, 2008); Evans E. Crawford, *The Hum: Call and Response in African American Preaching* (Nashville: Abingdon, 1995); Cleophus J. LaRue, *I Believe I'll Testify: The Art of African American Preaching* (Louisville: Westminster John Knox Press, 2011).

9. Hurston, *Jonah's Gourd Vine*, 174, 181.

10. Ibid.

11. Ibid., 174.

12. Ibid., 179.

13. Ibid., 174, 177.

14. Roxanne Mountford, *The Gendered Pulpit: Preaching in American Protestant Spaces*, Studies in Rhetorics and Feminisms (Carbondale: Southern Illinois University Press, 2003), 8–10.

15. Ibid., 19–20.

16. Zora Neale Hurston, *Their Eyes Were Watching God* (Philadelphia: J.B. Lippincott Co., 1937), 21.

17. See Toni Morrison, *Beloved: A Novel*, 1st Vintage International ed. (New York: Vintage International, 2004), 102–4; Judylin S. Ryan, "Spirituality and/as Ideology in Black Women's Literature: The Preaching of Maria Stewart and Baby Suggs, Holy," in *Women Preachers and Prophets through Two Millennia of Christianity*, ed. Beverly Mayne and Pamela J. Walker Kienzele (Berkeley: University of California Press, 1998).

18. See Mountford, *Gendered Pulpit*, 171.

19. Ibid., 103–4.

20. Ibid., 108 (emphasis added).

21. Teresa Fry Brown notes that African American women are less likely to be "groomed" from a young age into preaching ministries when

compared to African American men who have more immediately accessible mentors (see Teresa L. Fry Brown, *Weary Throats and New Songs: Black Women Proclaiming God's Word* [Nashville: Abingdon, 2003], 72).

3. Mining Life for Preaching

1. See John S. McClure, "The Cultural Code," chap. 4 in *The Four Codes of Preaching: Rhetorical Strategies* (Louisville: Westminster John Knox Press, 2003), 136–37.

2. Dale P. Andrews argues that the very nature of preaching in black worship spaces, in its best practices, holds together liberationist trajectories of black theological discourses and offers pastoral refuge (see Dale P. Andrews, *Practical Theology for Black Churches: Bridging Black Theology and African American Folk Religion* [Louisville: Westminster John Knox, 2002], 24–26).

3. For more on celebration, see Henry H. Mitchell, *Black Preaching: The Recovery of a Powerful Art* (Nashville: Abingdon, 1990); and Henry H. Mitchell, *Celebration and Experience in Preaching*, rev. ed. (Nashville: Abingdon, 2008).

4. See Frank Thomas, *They Like to Never Quit Praisin' God: The Role of Celebration in Preaching*, (Cleveland, OH: Pilgrim Press, 1997), 85.

5. Ibid., 98–104; Mitchell, *Black Preaching*, 119–22.

6. In a similar fashion to my description of stock formulas, Mitchell describes stock conclusions, noting these phrases are often a part of the celebratory moment of a sermon, without being limited solely to moments of celebration. See Mitchell, *Black Preaching*, 121.

7. See Henry Louis Gates, *The Signifying Monkey: A Theory of Afro-American Literary Criticism* (New York: Oxford University Press, 1988).

8. A lineage of work connects the expressions found in the blues and black music traditions as interpretations of faith and life, while arguing that these locales are where sacred dimensions displace what may be otherwise viewed as secular (see Kelly Brown Douglas, *Black Bodies and the*

Black Church: A Blues Slant [New York: Palgrave MacMillan, 2012]; James H. Cone, *The Spirituals and the Blues: An Interpretation* [Maryknoll, NY: Orbis, 1991]; Jon Michael Spencer, *Blues and Evil* [Knoxville: University of Tennessee Press, 1993]).

9. See Toni Morrison, *Beloved: A Novel*, 1st Vintage International ed. (New York: Vintage International, 2004).

10. See Teresa Fry Brown, *God Don't Like Ugly: African American Women Handing on Spiritual Values* (Nashville: Abingdon, 2000).

11. Eunjoo Mary Kim, *Women Preaching: Theology and Practice through the Ages* (Cleveland, OH: Pilgrim Press, 2004).

12. Ibid., 73.

13. Ibid., 74. Here Kim specifically engages the preaching of Hildegard of Bingen, Julian of Norwich, and Sor Juana Inés de la Cruz.

14. Ibid., 74–75.

15. Ibid., 75.

16. Kenneth Burke's identification theory describes the roles of symbols in persuasion and communication based on the proclivity of individuals to identify with symbols. Through the process of recognition and identification, cooperation is forged among the speaker, the listener, and the idea (see Kenneth Burke, *A Rhetoric of Motives* [Berkeley: University of California Press, 1969], 43).

17. Lenora Tubbs Tisdale, *Preaching as Local Theology and Folk Art* (Minneapolis: Fortress, 1997), 34.

18. Ibid., xiii, 43, 126.

19. Ibid., xiii, 124–25.

20. Ibid., xii.

21. Ibid., 64–77.

22. Ibid., xii, 38–39.

23. Ibid., 41–42, 45–46.

24. As Tisdale considers preaching a highly contextual act of communicating the gospel, she proposes a "con/text-to-sermon method" that keeps the context and congregation integral at every point of sermon development (see ibid., 99–121).

25. Ibid., 91.

26. Ibid., 76.

27. Ibid.

28. Ibid.

29. Mary Lin Hudson and Mary Donovan Turner, *Saved from Silence: Finding Women's Voice in Preaching* (St. Louis: Chalice Press, 1999), 12.

30. Ibid., 12–13.

31. Ibid., 12.

32. Tisdale, *Preaching as Local Theology and Folk Art*, 49–53.

33. Ibid., 132.

4. Recovering Sacred Texts for Preaching

1. See Gadamer's explication of a *fusion of horizons* in the process of interpretation (see Hans-Georg Gadamer, "The Ontology of the Work of Art and Its Hermeneutic Significance" and "Elements of a Theory of Hermeneutic Experience," chaps. 2 and 4 in *Truth and Method* (New York: Bloomsbury Academic, 2013), 316-18 [First published Sheed & Ward Ltd and Continuum Publishing Group, 1975].

2. Henry H. Mitchell, *Black Preaching: The Recovery of a Powerful Art* (Nashville: Abingdon, 1990), 59–60.

3. Gadamer argues for an interconnectedness among interpretation, meaning, and application (the concretization or instantiation of the meaning) (see Gadamer, *Truth and Method*, 317–19).

4. For more on the often complex relationship among the Bible, its inaccessible pages in the history of African Americans, and the aural-oral history of a people in search of the ethic the Bible espoused, see Allen Dwight Callahan, *The Talking Book: African Americans and the Bible* (New Haven, CT: Yale University Press, 2006).

5. See Mitchell, *Black Preaching,* 63-69.

6. See Chanequa Walker-Barnes, "To Carry Your Burden in the Heat of the Day," chap. 3 in *Too Heavy a Yoke* (Eugene: Cascade, 2014), 80-108.

7. I use the terms *women* and *the feminine* together as a note of the tradition of their usage, and not as a disregard of the limits and insufficiency in the binary gendered and default relational association between the two terms.

8. The preacher included a footnote indicating her adaption of "skin and kin" from a sermon by theologian and ethicist Katie G. Cannon, delivered at Washington National Cathedral in May 2007.

9. Carol Marie Norén, *The Woman in the Pulpit* (Nashville: Abingdon, 1991), 91, 102.

10. Ibid., 97-99.

11. Ibid., 100-102.

12. Ibid., 105.

13. Mitzi J. Smith, ed., *I Found God in Me: A Womanist Biblical Hermeneutics Reade*r (Eugene: Cascade, 2015), 4.

14. Ibid., 8.

15. Cleophus J. LaRue, *I Believe I'll Testify: The Art of African American Preaching* (Louisville: Westminster John Knox Press, 2011), 71-72; Gardner C. Taylor, *How Shall They Preach* (Elgin, IL: Progressive Baptist Pub. House, 1977), 60.

16. Anna Carter Florence, *Preaching as Testimony,* (Louisville: Westminster John Knox Press, 2007), 133-50.

17. LaRue proposes organizing imaginative thoughts into three categories: initial imaginative thoughts, informed imaginative thoughts, and enhanced imaginative thoughts (see LaRue, *I Believe I'll Testify*, 59–60, 72–73).

18. Florence, *Preaching as Testimony*, 133.

19. Ibid.

20. Ibid. (italics in the original text).

21. Ibid, 134.

22. Miguel A. De La Torre, *Reading the Bible from the Margins* (Maryknoll, NY: Orbis Books, 2002), 3–4.

23. Florence, *Preaching as Testimony*, 144–45 (Note: Italics were used in the original text.)

24. De La Torre, *Reading the Bible from the Margins*, 4.

25. Ibid.

26. Ibid., 4–5.

27. LaRue, *I Believe I'll Testify*, 76–7.

28. Ibid., 76.

29. For further reading on the preacher as ethnographer and interpreter of signs and symbols, see Lenora Tubbs Tisdale, *Preaching as Local Theology and Folk Art*, Fortress Resources for Preaching (Minneapolis: Fortress, 1997).

30. See Mae Gwendolyn Henderson, "Speaking in Tongues: Dialogics, Dialectics, and the Black Woman's Literary Tradition," in *Women, Autobiography, Theory: A Reader*, ed. Sidonie Smith and Julia Watson, *Wisconsin Studies in American Autobiography* (Madison: University of Wisconsin Press, 1998).

5. Finding "A Word from the Lord" for Today

1. Dale P. Andrews, "New to Whom?" Appendix A in *Preaching Prophetic Care: Building Bridges to Justice* (Eugene, OR: Wipf & Stock, 2018), 301.

2. John S. McClure, "Encountering the Word: Dale Andrews' Inductive Pedagogy for Prophetic Preaching," chap. 18 in *Preaching Prophetic Care: Building Bridges to Justice*, 184.

3. See Henry H. Mitchell, *Black Preaching: The Recovery of a Powerful Art* (Nashville: Abingdon, 1990), 96–97.

4. LaRue, *Heart of Black Preaching*, 12.

5. Ibid.

6. Samuel D. Proctor highlights the important and assumed role of a proposition to be given in his preaching methodology (see Samuel D. Proctor, *The Certain Sound of the Trumpet: Crafting a Sermon of Authority* [Valley Forge, PA: Judson Press, 1994], 33, 53).

7. See John S. McClure, *The Roundtable Pulpit: Where Leadership and Preaching Meet*, (Nashville: Abingdon, 1995) and Lucy Rose, *Sharing the Word: Preaching in the Roundtable Church* (Louisville: Westminster John Knox Press, 1997).

8. John S. McClure, "The Semantic Code" in *The Four Codes of Preaching: Rhetorical Strategies* (Louisville: Westminster John Knox Press, 2003), 57.

9. See Dale P. Andrews, "New to Whom?", 301; and Alyce M. McKenzie, "At the Intersection of *Actio Divina* and *Homo Performans*: Embodiment and Evocation," in *Performance in Preaching: Bringing the Sermon to Life*, ed. Jana Childers and Clayton J. Schmit (Grand Rapids: Baker Academic, 2008), 57.

10. Alyce M. McKenzie, "At the Intersection of *Actio Divina* and *Homo Performans*: Embodiment and Evocation," 58.

11. Miguel A. De La Torre, *Reading the Bible from the Margins* (Maryknoll, NY: Orbis Books, 2002), 38–39.

12. Ibid., 4.

13. Ibid., 40.

14. Cleophus J. LaRue, *I Believe I'll Testify: The Art of African American Preaching* (Louisville: Westminster John Knox Press, 2011), 76–77.

15. Walter Brueggemann, *The Prophetic Imagination* (Philadelphia: Fortress Press, 1978). Also see *The Practice of Prophetic Imagination: Preaching an Emancipatory Word* (Minneapolis: Fortress, 2012).

16. Brueggemann, *Prophetic Imagination*, 14–15.

17. Ibid., 16.

18. Ibid.

19. Ibid.

20. McKenzie, "At the Intersection of *Actio Divina* and *Homo Performans*," 57.

21. Ibid. As found in: Charles L. Bartow, *God's Human Speech: A Practical Theology of Proclamation* (Grand Rapids: W. B. Eerdmans, Pub., 1997), 111.

22. LaRue, *I Believe I'll Testify*, 64–65.

23. Walter Brueggemann, *The Word Militant: Preaching a Decentering Word* (Minneapolis: Fortress Press, 2007), 85.

24. John S. McClure, "Narrative and Preaching: Sorting It All Out," in *Journal for Preachers* 15, no. 1 (1991): 26.

25. Ibid.

26. See LaRue, *I Believe I'll Testify*, 64–68.

6. Locating God and Faith on the Ground

1. See John McClure, "The Theosymbolic Code," in *The Four Codes of Preaching: Rhetorical Strategies* (Louisville: Westminster John Knox, 2003), 93–135.

2. Ibid., 93–94.

3. For more on the theology as expressed through social practice, in response to on-the-ground needs and how this differs from construtive and systematic theology, see Kathryn Tannery, "The Nature and Task of Theology," ch. 4 in *Theories of Culture: A New Agenda for Theology* (Minneapolis: Fortress, 1997).

4. Kelly Brown Douglas, *What's Faith Got to Do with It? Black Bodies/Christian Souls* (Maryknoll, NY: Orbis Books, 2005), 201.

5. Ibid., 206–7.

6. Ibid., 205, 207.

7. See Brown Douglas, *What's Faith Got to Do with It?*, 3–38, 205.

8. Ibid., 204–5.

9. Ibid., 207.

10. See Jacquelyn Grant, *White Women's Christ and Black Women's Jesus: Feminist Christology and Womanist Response*, American Academy of Religion Academy Series (Atlanta: Scholars Press, 1989).

11. Cheryl Gilkes, "There Is a Work for Each One of Us: The Socio Theology of the Rev. Florence Spearing Randolph," in *How Long This Road: Race, Religion, and the Legacy of C. Eric Lincoln*, ed. Alton B. Pollard and L. H. Whelchel (New York: Palgrave Macmillan, 2003), 131–40.

12. Dale P. Andrews and Robert London Smith describe the black thematic universe as "the set of historical and cultural circumstances defining the situations and conditions that shape the experiences of reality for generations of Africans and Pan Africans" (see Dale P. Andrews and Robert London Smith, eds., *Black Practical Theology* (Waco, TX: Baylor University Press, 2015), 8.

13. For an in-depth discussion of theology, surrogacy, and black women, see Delores S. Williams, *Sisters in the Wilderness: The Challenge of Womanist Godtalk* (Maryknoll, NY: Orbis, 1993).

14. M. Shawn Copeland, "Wading through Many Sorrows: Toward a Theology of Suffering in a Womanist Perspective," in *A Troubling in My*

Soul: Womanist Perspectives on Evil and Suffering, ed. Emilie M. Townes (Maryknoll, NY: Orbis, 2005), 124–25.

15. Kelly Brown Douglas, *The Black Christ*, The Bishop Henry McNeal Turner Studies in North American Black Religion (Maryknoll, NY: Orbis, 1994), 107–9.

16. Ibid., 107–8.

17. McClure, "The Theosymbolic Code," 93–94.

18. Ibid.

19. Ibid., 93–95.

20. Ibid., 95–96.

21. Walter Brueggemann, *The Practice of Prophetic Imagination: Preaching an Emancipatory Word* (Minneapolis: Fortress, 2012), 85.

22. Lenora Tubbs Tisdale, *Preaching as Local Theology and Folk Art*, Fortress Resources for Preaching (Minneapolis: Fortress Press, 1997), 37–38.

23. See Cleophus J. LaRue, *I Believe I'll Testify: The Art of African American Preaching* (Louisville: Westminster John Knox Press, 2011), 59–60.

24. Leonora Tubbs Tisdale, *Prophetic Preaching: A Pastoral Approach*, 1st ed. (Louisville: Westminster John Knox Press, 2010), 11.

25. See Miguel A. De La Torre, *Reading the Bible from the Margins* (Maryknoll, NY: Orbis Books, 2002).

26. See Burton Z. Cooper and John S. McClure, *Claiming Theology in the Pulpit* (Louisville: Westminster John Knox Press, 2003), 31–35, 136; and McClure, *The Four Codes of Preaching: Rhetorical Strategies* (Louisville: Westminster John Knox Press, 2003), 130–32.

27. Dieter T. Hessel, *Social Ministry*, rev. ed. (Louisville: Westminster John Knox Press, 1992), 100–101.

28. Tisdale, *Prophetic Preaching*, 25–26.

www.ingramcontent.com/pod-product-compliance
Lightning Source LLC
Chambersburg PA
CBHW071957240426
43669CB00049B/2683